is that your final

answer?

is that your final

answer?

has been especially
written for Tesco
by Will Hersey

Published for
Tesco Stores Limited

First published 2000

Printed by
Lego Print SPA
Reproduction by
Graphic Ideas Studios

is that your final
answer?

Will Hersey

Mission Objectives

Are you capable of answering ten questions correctly? Yes.

Can you answer ten questions in a row, without getting any wrong? Maybe... Even if they're getting harder and harder each time? Mmmm...

This is the challenge that faces you... the only question now is, are you up to it?

rules

The book is divided into ten separate levels of difficulty, from one (very easy) to ten (very hard). Your aim is to correctly answer one question from each level, starting at level one and climbing to level ten. You can choose any question at random from each level. There are four possible answers given for each question – but only one is right. You can only progress to the next level with a correct answer – any mistake and your game is up. But if you want to go the distance, you might have to take some risks.

Take Twos

Take Twos allow you to remove two of the incorrect answers. Turn to the Take Two page at the end of each level and you'll be given the correct answer and one wrong answer. Every player is given two Take Twos at the start of each game. Use them wisely!

One Player

Pit your wits against the questions by working your way through the levels and seeing how far you can progress.

Two Players +

You can make things more competitive by challenging friends to a battle of minds! Take it in turns to ask the questions and see who can get to the highest level. If you think you can answer the question before being given the four possible answers, you can choose to gamble: if you are wrong your game is over, but if you are right you can skip the next level. For example, you can gamble on level two and go straight to level four, or gamble on level six and move on to level eight. However, to complete the game you must answer a level-ten question correctly. And always make sure you think carefully ... before giving your final answer.

level
one

take two

turn to page 20

01
Who had to contend with 40 thieves?

- A Ally McBeal
- B Ali Baba
- C Ali Shahid Mohammed
- D Ali G

02
What number is an ice cream and chocolate flake given?

- A One
- B Thirteen
- C Ninety-nine
- D One hundred

03
How many lives is a cat said to have?

- A None
- B Two
- C Five
- D Nine

04
What does a vampire drink?

- A Water
- B Wine
- C Blood
- D Lager top

05
What was Florence Nightingale?

- A A nurse
- B A singer
- C A scientist
- D A politician

06
In the 'Toy Story' films, what kind of toy is Woody?

- A A spaceman
- B A policeman
- C A cowboy
- D A racing driver

07
What is Egypt's most famous tourist attraction?

- A The Circles
- B The Rectangles
- C The Pyramids
- D The Cubes

08
In Roman numerals, what does X mean?

- A One
- B Ten
- C One hundred
- D Over 18s only

answers

turn to page 20

turn to page 20

09
What vegetable is used to make crisps?

- A Potato
- B Parsnip
- C Carrot
- D Cabbage

10
In which English city is Buckingham Palace?

- A Birmingham
- B London
- C Manchester
- D Norwich

11
What is a gondola?

- A A boat
- B A bird
- C A hat
- D A vegetable

12
What does the term thrice mean?

- A One time
- B Two times
- C Three times
- D A lady

13
Complete the title nf this play by Shakespeare:'Romeo and...'

- A Julie
- B Julia
- C Juliet
- D Bravo

14
Which country is famous for pasta, opera and pizza?

- A France
- B America
- C Wales
- D Italy

15
How were John, Paul, George and Ringo better known?

- A The Beatles
- B The Venga Boys
- C Take This
- D Scousezone

16
What is one hundredth of a metre called?

- A A fathom
- B A centimetre
- C A foot
- D An inch

      turn to page 20

11

t a k e t w o

turn to page 20

17
Which game ends with the word 'checkmate'?

- A Chess
- B Snap
- C Scrabble
- D Tennis

18
How long is a decade?

- A 5 years
- B 10 years
- C 50 years
- D 500 years

19
What kind of children did E. Nesbit write about?

- A Airport
- B Railway
- C Motorway
- D Bus depot

20
What is Chinese food normally cooked in?

- A A mok
- B A rok
- C A wok
- D A sok

21
Which video game follows the adventures of Lara Croft?

- A Crypt Rustler
- B Vault Invader
- C Tomb Raider
- D Catacomb Marauder

22
What might you get in a barber's?

- A A country coat
- B A haircut
- C A beard
- D A wire fence

23
Who does Clark Kent turn into?

- A Spiderman
- B Batman
- C Superman
- D Bananaman

24
What does an angler try to catch?

- A Colds
- B Balls
- C Fish
- D Chips

answers

turn to page 20

turn to page 20

25
Which is the shortest month of the year?

- A April
- B June
- C May
- D February

26
The foot of which animal is considered lucky?

- A A dove
- B A crow
- C A dog
- D A rabbit

27
Guy Fawkes was at the centre of which plot?

- A Gunpowder
- B Government
- C Firework
- D Vegetable

28
What legendary creature has only one eye?

- A Cyclops
- B Dracula
- C Werewolf
- D Nelson

29
Which day comes after Christmas Day?

- A Wrestling Day
- B Boxing Day
- C Sumo Day
- D Tae Kwando Day

30
Which doctor talks to the animals?

- A Who
- B Kildare
- C Doolittle
- D Jekyll

31
To whom did the Merry Men lend their support?

- A Henry VIII
- B Oliver Reed
- C Robin Hood
- D Zorro

32
What is the National Anthem of Great Britain?

- A Land of Hope & Glory
- B God Save Our Queen
- C Rule Britannia
- D Flower of Scotland

turn to page 20

take two

turn to page 20

33
What was the Spanish Armada?

- A A fleet of fighting ships
- B A fleet of cargo ships
- C A fleet of exploring ships
- D A fleet of fishing boats

34
In which Scottish lake is a famous monster said to lurk?

- A Loch Lomond
- B Loch Leven
- C Loch Ness
- D Loch N'key

35
Which bird symbolises peace?

- A A crow
- B A robin
- C An eagle
- D A dove

36
In which sport can the batsman be 'clean bowled by a yorker'?

- A Cricket
- B Tennis
- C Football
- D Bowls

37
Which planet is famous for its rings?

- A Mars
- B Diamond
- C Venus
- D Saturn

38
Which bird lends its name to one of Batman's enemies?

- A Albatross
- B Penguin
- C Flamingo
- D Chaffinch

39
Which bird is used for both carrying messages and racing?

- A A sparrow
- B A pigeon
- C A blackbird
- D A canary

40
What name is given to water that encircles a castle?

- A A keep
- B A drawbridge
- C A dungeon
- D A moat

answers

turn to page 20

41

What would you expect to find in a hamper?

- A Books
- B Food
- C Clothes
- D Tools

42

In which forest is Robin Hood said to have lived?

- A The New Forest
- B The National Forest
- C Sherwood Forest
- D Epping Forest

43

What kind of animal is the film character 'Babe'?

- A A cow
- B A dog
- C A pig
- D A sheep

44

What is another name for the Skull and Crossbones flag?

- A The Jolly Roger
- B The Contented Jeremy
- C The Happy Gordon
- D The Satisfied Graham

45

What is a siesta?

- A A three-piece band
- B An afternoon lie-down
- C A Mexican bull-ring
- D A street party

46

What was Winston Churchill?

- A A scientist
- B A cricketer
- C A General
- D Prime Minister

47

How many colours are there in the rainbow?

- A Five
- B Six
- C Seven
- D Eight

48

Which word can go before station, man and ship?

- A Railway
- B Space
- C Work
- D Play

answers

turn to page 20

15

49
Who had adventures in Wonderland?

- A Agnes
- B Alice
- C Dorothy
- D Miriam

50
What was an abacus used for?

- A Warfare
- B Transport
- C Calculations
- D Communication

51
Where would you look through portholes?

- A On a boat
- B In a wine cellar
- C In an aquarium
- D In a nightclub

52
Which colour is created by mixing red and yellow?

- A Banana
- B Orange
- C Apple
- D Pineapple

53
What is the largest animal in the world?

- A Blue whale
- B Giraffe
- C Giant panda
- D Godzilla

54
Sausages and batter combine to make which dish?

- A Snake-in-the-grass
- B Frog-in-the-throat
- C Toad-in-the-hole
- D Sausage-in-the-batter

55
Which king did the Knights of the Round Table serve?

- A Ralph
- B Richard
- C Alfred
- D Arthur

56
What name is given to an angle of 90°?

- A Left
- B Right
- C Straight on
- D Next door but one

take two

turn to ● page 20

57

What kind of animal is the film character Dumbo?

- A A mouse
- B A pig
- C An elephant
- D A lion

58

What name is given to the top of a volcano?

- A Summit
- B Peak
- C Crater
- D Crust

59

According to the proverb, what is a bird in the hand worth?

- A One in the tree
- B Two in the bush
- C Three on the roof
- D Four in the sky

60

What is Bordeaux in France most famous for producing?

- A Cheese
- B Art
- C Wine
- D Footballers

61

What is Crufts?

- A A cat show
- B A flower show
- C A car show
- D A dog show

62

Which battle did the Bayeux Tapestry chronicle?

- A The Battle of Waterloo
- B The Battle of Trafalgar
- C The Battle of Hastings
- D The Battle of Handicraft

63

How many times did Henry VIII marry?

- A Twice
- B Six
- C Ten
- D Never

64

The Tour de France is a race for which type of transport?

- A Cars
- B Bicycles
- C Motorbikes
- D Horses

answers turn to ● page 20

65

Which island did Robert Louis Stevenson write about?

- A Coral Island
- B Treasure Island
- C Dolphin Island
- D Thousand Island

66

How much is a 'grand'?

- A £100
- B £500
- C £1,000
- D £10,000

67

Which word can go before made, cooking and town?

- A French
- B Market
- C Home
- D Hand

68

What is a technophobe afraid of?

- A Dance music
- B Studying
- C Telephones
- D Technology

69

Chicken vindaloo is a classic dish from which country?

- A China
- B Thailand
- C India
- D Scotland

70

Which vegetable did Sir Walter Raleigh introduce to Britain?

- A Onion
- B Potato
- C Mushroom
- D Marrow

71

Which is the highest mountain in the world?

- A Ben Nevis
- B K2
- C Kilimanjaro
- D Everest

72

What is a deerstalker?

- A A hat
- B A hunter
- C A gun
- D A jacket

73
What does an olive branch represent?

- A Peace
- B War
- C Love
- D Food

74
What was Moby Dick?

- A A monster
- B An elephant
- C A dinosaur
- D A whale

75
Which fruit has varieties called Braeburn, Cox and Pippin?

- A Pear
- B Apple
- C Peach
- D Plum

76
The four-leafed variety of which plant is considered lucky?

- A Ivy
- B Holly
- C Clover
- D Dock

77
Which tree do conkers come from?

- A Oak
- B Horse chestnut
- C Willow
- D Sycamore

78
What did the Biro brothers invent?

- A The vacuum cleaner
- B The mobile phone
- C The ballpoint pen
- D The supermarket

79
Whose headquarters are called Scotland Yard?

- A The Fire Brigade
- B The Flying Squad
- C The Ambulance service
- D The Metropolitan police

80
In which country is the Leaning Tower of Pisa?

- A Spain
- B Italy
- C France
- D Portugal

answers

turn to page 20

19

take two

Check your options to the questions below

answers

level
two

2

take two

Turn to page 32

01
Which city is known as the Big Apple?

- A Amsterdam
- B Rio de Janeiro
- C Barcelona
- D New York

02
How are Caspar, Melchior and Balthazar better known?

- A The Three Wise Men
- B The three stooges
- C The Three Musketeers
- D Westlife

03
What is a group of lions called?

- A An ego
- B A pride
- C A boast
- D An arrogance

04
What is traditionally 'thrown in' as a sign of defeat?

- A The towel
- B The bucket
- C A white flag
- D A gauntlet

05
Which football club is nicknamed the Gunners?

- A Chelsea
- B Millwall
- C Tottenham
- D Arsenal

06
Which word can go before mate, shape, and yard?

- A Work
- B Ship
- C Car
- D Best

07
At what weight did Lennox Lewis become a world champion?

- A Flyweight
- B Welterweight
- C Super middleweight
- D Heavyweight

08
What caused the Titanic to sink?

- A A torpedo
- B Kate Winslett
- C An iceberg
- D A tidal Wave

answers

Turn to page 32

09
Where are coins and banknotes made?

- A Bank
- B Mint
- C Bureau de change
- D On trees

10
Near which city is Euro Disney?

- A Paris
- B Barcelona
- C Munich
- D Milan

11
"Please sir, can I have some more" is a line from which novel?

- A Bleak House
- B David Copperfield
- C Great Expectations
- D Oliver Twist

12
What do the opposite sides of a dice add up to?

- A Six
- B Seven
- C Eight
- D Nine

13
Where is charity said to begin?

- A At work
- B At school
- C At home
- D In the garden

14
What is a risotto's principal ingredient?

- A Pasta
- B Rice
- C Potato
- D Couscous

15
For which activity is Rip Van Winkle famous?

- A Writing
- B Eating
- C Drinking
- D Sleeping

16
Which ingredient is used to raise bread?

- A Baking powder
- B Flour
- C Yeast
- D Salt

answers

Turn to page 32

take two

Turn to page 32

17
What are diapers to an American?

- A Nappies
- B Car boots
- C Cheques
- D Mobile phones

18
What does the e in e-mail stand for?

- A Electric
- B Excuse
- C Electronic
- D External

19
What is measured in reams?

- A Sleep
- B Paper
- C Butter
- D Horses

20
Where does rubber come from?

- A Trees
- B Rock
- C Tyres
- D Plastic

21
What song is traditionally sung on New Year's Eve?

- A Rule Britannia
- B Auld Lang Syne
- C All Creatures Great and Small
- D Kum ba yah

22
What name is given to someone who gives evidence in court?

- A Judge
- B Lawyer
- C Juror
- D Witness

23
What door-length windows often open into a garden?

- A Italian
- B German
- C French
- D Spanish

24
How many sides does a cube have?

- A Four
- B Six
- C Twelve
- D Twentyfour

answers

turn to page 32

25

When is the 'witching hour'?

- ◆A Noon
- ◆B Dusk
- ◆C Midnight
- ◆D 3.37 pm

26

What percentage of 1km is 400m?

- ◆A 25 %
- ◆B 55 %
- ◆C 40 %
- ◆D 70 %

27

What kind of bomb was used during the Dambusters Raid?

- ◆A Bouncing
- ◆B Hydrogen
- ◆C Petrol
- ◆D Carpet

28

Which bird lays its eggs in other birds' nests?

- ◆A A wren
- ◆B A sparrow
- ◆C A cuckoo
- ◆D A starling

29

What is salmonella?

- ◆A A fish dish
- ◆B A bacteria
- ◆C A flowering shrub
- ◆D A pudding

30

What does the U in UFO stand for?

- ◆A Unreported
- ◆B Unidentified
- ◆C Unknown
- ◆D Unproven

31

What kind of holiday is spent doing your usual job?

- ◆A Busman's
- ◆B Workman's
- ◆C Dustman's
- ◆D Journeyman's

32

What pursuit involves descending a cliff on a rope?

- ◆A Parascending
- ◆B Hang-gliding
- ◆C Bungee-jumping
- ◆D Abseiling

answers
turn to page 32

25

33

What is a collection of five musicians called?

- A A cinquet
- B A fiver
- C A septet
- D A quintet

34

What is wattle and daub traditionally used for?

- A Sculpting
- B Model-making
- C House building
- D Painting

35

What do decibels measure?

- A Strength
- B Loudness
- C Brightness
- D Thickness

36

What is a matador's place of work?

- A A hospital
- B A zoo
- C A bull-ring
- D A hotel

37

In which language did the Romans communicate?

- A Italian
- B Latin
- C Ancient Greek
- D Esperanto

38

What is a kayak?

- A A canoe
- B A mountain goat
- C A Muslim prayer mat
- D A jungle guide

39

Where do Joey, Chandler, Monica and Rachel live?

- A Paris
- B London
- C Los Angeles
- D New York

40

Which banned pollutants are said to damage the ozone layer?

- A CFCs
- B FCDs
- C CBCs
- D DFDs

26

answers

turn to   page 32

take two

turn to page 32

41

How many people normally make up a jury?

- A Nine
- B Fifteen
- C Twelve
- D One

42

What is the opposite of cowardice?

- A Integrity
- B Courage
- C Power
- D Intelligence

43

To which instrument family does the flute belong?

- A Brass
- B Wind
- C String
- D Addams

44

What is the name of the boy who helps ET to get home?

- A Stephen
- B Todd
- C Elliot
- D Brad

45

Who created the famous detective, Sherlock Holmes?

- A H. G. Wells
- B Sir Arthur Conan Doyle
- C Charles Dickens
- D Dr. Watson

46

Where is 'The Lion, the Witch and the Wardrobe' set?

- A Atlantis
- B Narnia
- C The Snow Cavern
- D The Furniture Warehouse

47

Who invented the telephone?

- A Bell
- B Baird
- C Graham
- D Telecom

48

What currency is used in the Netherlands?

- A Amstel
- B Goey
- C Inglander
- D Guilder

answers

turn to page 32

49

Who was the first president of the United States?

- A Abraham Lincoln
- B George Washington
- C Theodore Roosevelt
- D Uncle Sam

50

'Waterloo' and 'Mama Mia' were hit records for which group

- A ABBA
- B The Bay City Rollers
- C Slade
- D Bucks Fizz

51

What is known as 'the Scottish play'?

- A 'Ivanhoe'
- B 'King Lear'
- C 'Macbeth'
- D 'Braveheart'

52

Which word can go before travel, zone, and piece?

- A Time
- B Space
- C World
- D Hair

53

In which London borough is the Millennium Dome?

- A Greenwich
- B Westminster
- C Lambeth
- D Hammersmith

54

What are trees that lose their leaves in autumn called?

- A Evergreen
- B Seasonal
- C Deciduous
- D Autumnal

55

Where was the Tree of Knowledge?

- A Alan Titchmarsh's allotment
- B Hanging Gardens of Babylon
- C The Secret Garden
- D Garden of Eden

56

In which card game might you use the term 'royal flush'?

- A Contract Bridge
- B Poker
- C Pontoon
- D Snap

take two

turn to page 32

57
What is an abattoir?

- A A water reserve
- B A slaughterhouse
- C A bird sanctuary
- D A Swedish music festival

58
What was Yuri Gagarin the first person to do?

- A Swim the Atlantic
- B Run a four-minute mile
- C Climb Mount Everest
- D Go into space

59
Which river runs through Paris?

- A Danube
- B Seine
- C Loire
- D Dordogne

60
What does a ballerina wear on stage?

- A A tutu
- B A desmond
- C A friller
- D A bussell

61
How many Deadly Sins are there said to be?

- A Seven
- B Five
- C Twelve
- D Ten

62
Who lives in the Emerald City?

- A Spiderman
- B St. Patrick
- C The Wizard of Oz
- D Dan Dare

63
How many sides does a pentagon have?

- A Five
- B Seven
- C Nine
- D Many

64
Where might you use secateurs?

- A In the garage
- B In the kitchen
- C In the garden
- D In the bathroom

answers

turn to page 32

turn to   page 32

65
Which vegetable has a variety called King Edward?

- A Onion
- B Parsnip
- C Potato
- D Carrot

66
Which name is used to signal the end of a CB radio broadcast?

- A Maurice
- B Roger
- C Winston
- D Stanley

67
Who created the characters Hercule Poirot and Miss Marple?

- A Patricia Cornwell
- B Ruth Rendell
- C Agatha Christie
- D Sir Arthur Conan Doyle

68
In which English county are the Broads?

- A Yorkshire
- B Essex
- C Suffolk
- D Norfolk

69
What name is given to a man's evening stubble?

- A 3 o'clock shadow
- B 5 o'clock shadow
- C 7 o'clock shadow
- D Moonlight shadow

70
In 'Gulliver's Travels' where did a race of miniature people live?

- A Lilliput
- B Hilliput
- C Filliput
- D Halibut

71
Which two countries was Hadrian's Wall built to divide?

- A England and Scotland
- B Germany and Austria
- C USA and Mexico
- D France and Spain

72
Who wrote 'Hamlet, Prince of Denmark'?

- A William Wordsworth
- B Oscar Wilde
- C William Shakespeare
- D Robbie Williams

answers turn to page 32

turn to page 32

73
What is ex-President Mandela of South Africa's first name?

- ◆A Nelson
- ◆B Neilsen
- ◆C Neil
- ◆D Nell

74
What is said to be the most important meal of the day?

- ◆A Breakfast
- ◆B Lunch
- ◆C Dinner
- ◆D The next one

75
During which war did The Blitz take place?

- ◆A World War One
- ◆B World War Two
- ◆C The Crimean War
- ◆D The English Civil War

76
What is the opposite of perfect?

- ◆A Inperfect
- ◆B Unperfect
- ◆C Imperfect
- ◆D Perfectless

77
Whose paintings include 'Self-Portrait with Bandaged Ear'?

- ◆A Picasso's
- ◆B Michelangelo's
- ◆C Van Gogh's
- ◆D Onéar's

78
Complete the phrase: 'A friend in need is a friend...'?

- ◆A To take heed
- ◆B Indeed
- ◆C To feed
- ◆D To avoid

79
Which country was once ruled by Tsars?

- ◆A Germany
- ◆B China
- ◆C Russia
- ◆D Italy

80
What are animals that live on both land and water called?

- ◆A Reptiles
- ◆B Amphibians
- ◆C Omnivores
- ◆D Mammals

turn to page 32

31

take two

Check your options to the questions below

page 22	page 23	page 24	page 25	page 26
01 CD	09 AB	17 AD	25 BC	33 AD
02 AC	10 AB	18 CD	26 AC	34 AC
03 BC	11 CD	19 BC	27 AB	35 AB
04 AC	12 BC	20 AD	28 AC	36 CD
05 CD	13 AC	21 BD	29 BD	37 AB
06 AB	14 BC	22 BD	30 BC	38 AC
07 CD	15 AD	23 CD	31 AD	39 CD
08 AC	16 BC	24 AB	32 AD	40 AD

page 27	page 28	page 29	page 30	page 31
41 AC	49 AB	57 AB	65 CD	73 AC
42 AB	50 AB	58 AD	66 BD	74 AB
43 AB	51 BC	59 BC	67 BC	75 AB
44 BC	52 AB	60 AD	68 CD	76 BC
45 AB	53 AC	61 AD	69 BC	77 AC
46 BC	54 CD	62 CD	70 AC	78 AB
47 AC	55 BD	63 AC	71 AD	79 BC
48 AD	56 BC	64 AC	72 AC	80 AB

answers

page 22	page 23	page 24	page 25	page 26
01 D	09 B	17 A	25 C	33 D
02 A	10 A	18 C	26 C	34 C
03 B	11 D	19 B	27 A	35 B
04 A	12 B	20 A	28 C	36 C
05 D	13 C	21 B	29 B	37 B
06 B	14 B	22 D	30 B	38 A
07 D	15 D	23 C	31 A	39 D
08 C	16 C	24 B	32 D	40 A

page 27	page 28	page 29	page 30	page 31
41 C	49 B	57 B	65 C	73 A
42 B	50 A	58 D	66 B	74 A
43 B	51 C	59 B	67 C	75 B
44 C	52 A	60 A	68 D	76 C
45 B	53 A	61 A	69 B	77 C
46 B	54 C	62 C	70 A	78 B
47 A	55 D	63 A	71 A	79 C
48 D	56 B	64 C	72 C	80 B

level
three

3

take two
turn to page 44

01

What does the first D in DVD stand for?

- ◆ A Disc
- ◆ B Digital
- ◆ C Disappointing
- ◆ D Dated

02

Which crop is grown in a paddy field?

- ◆ A Tea
- ◆ B Coffee
- ◆ C Potato
- ◆ D Rice

03

How many inches are there in a foot?

- ◆ A 4
- ◆ B 6
- ◆ C 12
- ◆ D 20

04

Who became British Prime Minister in 1990?

- ◆ A John Major
- ◆ B Edward Heath
- ◆ C Margaret Thatcher
- ◆ D Neil Kinnock

05

Which breed of dog is also known as a German Shepherd?

- ◆ A Labrador
- ◆ B Dalmatian
- ◆ C Alsatian
- ◆ D Jack Russell

06

What is the TA?

- ◆ A Transport Authority
- ◆ B Territorial Army
- ◆ C Traindrivers Association
- ◆ D Tunisian Airforce

07

What name is given to the path an electric current takes?

- ◆ A A circuit
- ◆ B A route
- ◆ C A board
- ◆ D Wiring

08

What is the female version of a peacock called?

- ◆ A A partridge
- ◆ B A turtledove
- ◆ C A grouse
- ◆ D A peahen

answers
turn to page 44

09

What is the capital city of Northern Ireland?

- ◆ A Omagh
- ◆ B Belfast
- ◆ C Dublin
- ◆ D Londonderry

10

Which organisation protects the rights of animals in the UK?

- ◆ A The NSPCC
- ◆ B The RSPCA
- ◆ C The WWF
- ◆ D RSVP

11

Which French game is played with metal balls?

- ◆ A Boules
- ◆ B Natation
- ◆ C Babyfoot
- ◆ D Kerplunk

12

What type of food is 'ciabatta'?

- ◆ A Cheese
- ◆ B Ham
- ◆ C Bread
- ◆ D Pasta

13

What do hydrogen and oxygen combine to form?

- ◆ A Carbon dioxide
- ◆ B Helium
- ◆ C Water
- ◆ D Cider

14

Which motorway encircles London?

- ◆ A M1
- ◆ B M4
- ◆ C M60
- ◆ D M25

15

In French cooking, which fruit is traditionally eaten with duck?

- ◆ A Apple
- ◆ B Pear
- ◆ C Orange
- ◆ D Plum

16

How many tasks did Hercules have to complete?

- ◆ A Seven
- ◆ B Twelve
- ◆ C Twenty
- ◆ D Ten

turn to page 44

17
What are the Academy Awards better known as?

- A The Emmys
- B The Baftas
- C The Brits
- D The Oscars

18
What did Isaac Newton discover when an apple fell on his head?

- A Acceleration
- B Gravity
- C Terminal velocity
- D Pain

19
What were Roman galleys?

- A Weapons
- B Ships
- C Prisons
- D Torture devices

20
In New Zealand, which animals outnumber people?

- A Sheep
- B Cows
- C Rabbits
- D Chickens

21
Which organisation has the motto 'Faster, Longer, Higher'?

- A The Girl Guides
- B The Olympics
- C The Foreign Legion
- D The Genetic Research Council

22
What was it illegal to buy and sell during Prohibition?

- A Food
- B Cigarettes
- C Alcohol
- D Machine guns

23
What is a taxidermist's area of expertise?

- A Skin care
- B Boat building
- C Overcharging passengers
- D Animal stuffing

24
How many is a 'baker's dozen'?

- A Eleven
- B Twelve
- C Thirteen
- D Fourteen

answers

turn to page 44

take two
turn to · page 44

25
What name is given to a blind consisting of horizontal slats?

- A Roman
- B Florentine
- C Venetian
- D Milanese

26
What is the capital of Portugal?

- A Lisbon
- B Madrid
- C Seville
- D Grenada

27
Which film begins with the words 'A long, long, time ago'?

- A 'Jurassic Park'
- B 'Star Wars'
- C 'Spartacus'
- D 'Blade Runner'

28
Which range of mountains surrounds Switzerland?

- A Pyrenees
- B Dolomites
- C Alps
- D Urals

29
What is a claustrophobe afraid of?

- A Confined spaces
- B Open spaces
- C Living spaces
- D Parking spaces

30
In which of the arts was Alfred Hitchcock famous?

- A Film
- B Poetry
- C Theatre
- D Jazz

31
Which colour appears with red on the Spanish flag?

- A Blue
- B Yellow
- C Orange
- D White

32
Who defeated Napoleon at the Battle of Waterloo?

- A Nelson
- B Montgomery
- C Churchill
- D Wellington

answers
turn to · page 44

turn to **e** page 44

33
The Hershey company operates in which industry?

- A Agriculture
- B Banking
- C Confectionery
- D Media

34
Who is considered the founder of modern communism?

- A Groucho Marx
- B Harpo Marx
- C Karl Marx
- D Zeppo Marx

35
If someone has an Achilles' heel, what do they have?

- A A hidden strength
- B A personal weakness
- C A lucky nature
- D A dodgy ankle

36
In which country is the Great Barrier Reef?

- A Greece
- B Mexico
- C Australia
- D Japan

37
Which animal's name describes a punch to the back of the head?

- A Rabbit punch
- B Hare punch
- C Wolf punch
- D Dragon punch

38
What was Pandora not allowed to open?

- A Her door
- B Her heart
- C Her box
- D Her mind

39
What is a mandolin?

- A An insect
- B A language
- C A fruit
- D A musical instrument

40
Which country's flag is called the 'tricolore'?

- A Italy's
- B Germany's
- C France's
- D Belgium's

answers turn to page 44

41

What are petits pois?

- A Chips
- B Beans
- C Peas
- D Sweetcorn

42

What is the name for the main body of an aircraft?

- A Carriage
- B Cockpit
- C Fuselage
- D Delta

43

With what colour was WWI pilot Baron Von Richtofen associated?

- A Black
- B Red
- C Blue
- D Yellow

44

Which Greek author is noted for his fables?

- A Homer
- B Aesop
- C Socrates
- D Prince Philip

45

What is a debacle?

- A A disaster
- B A celebration
- C A rest period
- D An understanding

46

How is a collection of geese better known?

- A A flock
- B A gang
- C A gaggle
- D A group

47

What food has varieties called iceberg, cos and lollo rosso?

- A Onion
- B Lettuce
- C Cucumber
- D Potato

48

What is the first book of the Bible called?

- A Revelations
- B Genesis
- C Exodus
- D Author's note

answers

turn to page 44

39

49
Where is the Sea of Tranquillity?

- ◆ A Nepal
- ◆ B The Moon
- ◆ C The human body
- ◆ D Antarctica

50
Rice belongs to which food group?

- ◆ A Protein
- ◆ B Mineral
- ◆ C Fat
- ◆ D Carbohydrate

51
What is the Chancellor of the Exchequer responsible for?

- ◆ A Health
- ◆ B Finance
- ◆ C Foreign Affairs
- ◆ D Law and order

52
What is the name of the Corrs' lead singer?

- ◆ A Andrea
- ◆ B Amy
- ◆ C Alison
- ◆ D Amanda

53
What is the national symbol of Canada?

- ◆ A The moose
- ◆ B The mountie
- ◆ C The maple leaf
- ◆ D The grizzly bear

54
Where was apartheid used to divide the country by race?

- ◆ A South Africa
- ◆ B America
- ◆ C Zimbabwe
- ◆ D Russia

55
Whose tomb did Howard Carter discover?

- ◆ A Cleopatra's
- ◆ B Hiawatha's
- ◆ C Lord Lucan's
- ◆ D Tutankhamen's

56
How many lines of verse make up a limerick?

- ◆ A Three
- ◆ B Four
- ◆ C Five
- ◆ D Six

turn to page 44

57
What kind of boat
has two hulls?

- A A schooner
- B A cruiser
- C A catamaran
- D A topper

58
Over what distance was Roger
Bannister a record breaker?

- A 100 metres
- B 1 mile
- C 1,500 metres
- D Marathon

59
The Pope is the head
of which church?

- A Protestant
- B Muslim
- C Anglican
- D Roman Catholic

60
Who is the author of the
Harry Potter books?

- A J. D. Salinger
- B J. K Galbraith
- C J. M. Barrie
- D J. K. Rowling

61
What are people who sit in on
exams to stop cheating called?

- A Invigorators
- B Invigilators
- C Integraters
- D Interrogaters

62
What do climbers use
to improve their grip?

- A Clampons
- B Crimpons
- C Crampons
- D Crampins

63
In which city can
you visit Red Square?

- A Moscow
- B Berlin
- C Vienna
- D Reading

64
If you don't eat eggs, meat or
dairy products, what are you?

- A A herbivore
- B A vegetarian
- C A vegan
- D A vegemite

turn to page 44

take two

turn to (e) page 44

65
Who is described as an 'indomitable Gaulish warrior'?

- A Tintin
- B D'Artagnan
- C Asterix
- D Depardieu

66
Which theory is used to describe the creation of the universe?

- A The Big Bang
- B The Ice Age
- C Parkinson's Law
- D The New Dawn

67
What must your computer have to get online?

- A A scanner
- B A modem
- C A DVD drive
- D A mouse

68
Where were the 1996 Summer Olympics held?

- A Barcelona
- B Tokyo
- C Portsmouth
- D Atlanta

69
What are there 100 of in one German mark?

- A Pfennig
- B Centimes
- C Pennies
- D Kroner

70
What was the escapologist Houdini's first name?

- A Heathcliff
- B Harry
- C Hector
- D Colin

71
What is the name for a young hare?

- A A harridon
- B A leveret
- C A rabbit
- D A harem

72
Where is the US computer industry based?

- A Death Valley
- B Napa Valley
- C Silicon Valley
- D Frankie Valley

answers turn to page 44

turn to page 44

73
What is acupuncture?

- A A form of torture
- B A medical treatment
- C A breathing technique
- D A bad flat tyre

74
What does the M in CD-ROM stand for?

- A Modem
- B Mobile
- C Memory
- D Menthol

75
What colour did Henry Ford want all his cars to be?

- A Black
- B White
- C Silver
- D Banana yellow

76
Madrid is the capital of which country?

- A Italy
- B Spain
- C Portugal
- D Switzerland

77
What kind of key is used tn tighten screws?

- A Mark
- B Clive
- C Allan
- D Terry

78
What is the square root of 169?

- A Eleven
- B Thirteen
- C Fifteen
- D Seventeen

79
Which actor starred as James Bond in the film Goldeneye?

- A Roger Moore
- B George Lazenby
- C Pierce Brosnan
- D Sean Connery

80
In which sport do you play under Queensberry Rules?

- A Boxing
- B Wrestling
- C Rugby Union
- D Polo

turn to page 44

take two

Check your options to the questions below

page 34		page 35		page 36		page 37		page 38	
01	AB	09	BC	17	BD	25	AC	33	BC
02	AD	10	BC	18	BC	26	AC	34	AC
03	BC	11	AB	19	BC	27	BD	35	AB
04	AD	12	AC	20	AD	28	BC	36	AC
05	AC	13	AC	21	BC	29	AC	37	AC
06	AB	14	CD	22	BC	30	AC	38	BC
07	AC	15	CD	23	AD	31	BD	39	CD
08	BD	16	BD	24	CD	32	AD	40	AC

page 39		page 40		page 41		page 42		page 43	
41	CD	49	AB	57	AC	65	BC	73	AB
42	AC	50	AD	58	BD	66	AD	74	AC
43	AB	51	BD	59	AD	67	AB	75	AB
44	AB	52	AD	60	CD	68	AD	76	BC
45	AC	53	BC	61	AB	69	AD	77	AC
46	BC	54	AC	62	AC	70	AB	78	BC
47	BC	55	AD	63	AC	71	AB	79	CD
48	AB	56	CD	64	BC	72	BC	80	AC

answers

page 34		page 35		page 36		page 37		page 38	
01	B	09	B	17	D	25	A	33	C
02	D	10	B	18	B	26	A	34	C
03	C	11	B	19	B	27	B	35	B
04	A	12	C	20	A	28	C	36	C
05	C	13	C	21	B	29	A	37	A
06	B	14	D	22	C	30	A	38	C
07	A	15	C	23	D	31	B	39	D
08	D	16	B	24	C	32	D	40	C

page 39		page 40		page 41		page 42		page 43	
41	C	49	B	57	C	65	C	73	B
42	C	50	D	58	B	66	A	74	C
43	B	51	B	59	D	67	B	75	A
44	B	52	A	60	D	68	D	76	B
45	A	53	C	61	B	69	A	77	C
46	C	54	A	62	C	70	B	78	B
47	B	55	D	63	A	71	B	79	C
48	B	56	C	64	C	72	C	80	A

level
four

turn to page 56

01
Where is Traitors' Gate?

- A The London Dungeons
- B The Tower of London
- C Madame Tussaud's
- D The Houses of Parliament

02
What is known as the 'sport of kings'?

- A Real Tennis
- B Horse racing
- C Polo
- D Fox hunting

03
Which country forms the Iberian peninsula with Spain?

- A Italy
- B France
- C Portugal
- D Morocco

04
Who was the first person to reach the South Pole?

- A Robert Scott
- B Edmund Hillary
- C Edmund Mallory
- D Roald Amundsen

05
What does 'auf wiedersehen' mean?

- A Goodbye
- B Hello
- C Thank you
- D Good luck

06
Who came up with the theory of relativity?

- A Charles Darwin
- B Galileo
- C Albert Einstein
- D Archimedes

07
What is an enchilada?

- A A spicy dish
- B A US rodent
- C A Brazilian dance
- D An incendiary device

08
What is a general practitioner's area of expertise?

- A Law
- B Medicine
- C Religion
- D Politics

answers turn to page 56

turn to page 56

09
In a republic, who is normally the head of state?

- A The monarch
- B The Prime Minister
- C The President
- D The Emperor

10
What did Britain hand over control of in 1998?

- A Hong Kong
- B Gibraltar
- C The Falkland Islands
- D Australia

11
What colour elephant describes an unwanted object?

- A Pink
- B Blue
- C White
- D Silver

12
Which area of the body do palpitations affect?

- A The brain
- B The heart
- C The stomach
- D The legs

13
Which rugby team performs the 'Haka' before every match?

- A South Africa
- B Fiji
- C Western Samoa
- D New Zealand

14
What is Trinidad's capital city?

- A Port of Portugal
- B Port of Spain
- C Port of Italy
- D Port of England

15
What is the coil that heats water inside kettles called?

- A The component
- B The factor
- C The element
- D The unit

16
What is known as the home of cricket?

- A Lord's
- B Canterbury
- C The Oval
- D Edgbaston

answers turn to page 56

47

take two

turn to page 56

17
Where were fireworks invented?

- A Egypt
- B China
- C Peru
- D North Korea

18
The eruption of Vesuvius buried which Roman city?

- A Correalanum
- B Londinium
- C Pompeii
- D Lutetia

19
What is a hydrophobe afraid of?

- A Water
- B Illness
- C Flying
- D Questions

20
In a car, where is the klaxon?

- A The engine
- B The exhaust
- C The tyre
- D The steering wheel

21
What does 'circa' mean?

- A Exactly
- B Approximately
- C Scientifically
- D Unintentionally

22
Which 'Tales' did Geoffrey Chaucer write?

- A Canterbury
- B Winchester
- C Wessex
- D Old Wives'

23
If you ordered 'grenouilles' in a restaurant, what would you eat?

- A Snails
- B Garlic mushrooms
- C Frogs' legs
- D Seaweed

24
What is Yorkshire's popular valley region called?

- A The Moors
- B The Pennines
- C The Dales
- D The Waynes

answers

turn to page 56

turn to page 56

25

Which form of transport ended with the Hindenberg disaster?

- ◆A Steam train
- ◆B Zeppelin
- ◆C Tram
- ◆D Sedan chair

26

What does the seasoning paprika come from?

- ◆A Chillies
- ◆B Peppers
- ◆C Flowers
- ◆D Packets

27

Which English king signed the Magna Carta?

- ◆A Richard
- ◆B William
- ◆C Henry
- ◆D John

28

What substances, found in food, are needed for good health?

- ◆A Endorphins
- ◆B E numbers
- ◆C Preservatives
- ◆D Nutrients

29

Which country is the island of Corfu a part of?

- ◆A Italy
- ◆B Spain
- ◆C Greece
- ◆D Turkey

30

Which musician called his home Graceland?

- ◆A Elvis Presley
- ◆B Frank Sinatra
- ◆C Buddy Holly
- ◆D Liberace

31

Which river flows through Nottingham?

- ◆A Humber
- ◆B Tees
- ◆C Trent
- ◆D Nile

32

What are motorways called in Germany?

- ◆A Autostrades
- ◆B Autobahns
- ◆C Autovistas
- ◆D Check points

turn to page 56

turn to page 56

33
What is a kiln?

- A A pottery oven
- B A Church basement
- C A Scottish shawl
- D An industrial tool

34
What is the United Kingdom's national speed limit?

- A 30 mph
- B 40 mph
- C 60 mph
- D 70 mph

35
What is the daytime profession of the adventurer Indiana Jones?

- A Historian
- B Archaeologist
- C Antiques dealer
- D Private detective

36
What is 'petit dejeuner'?

- A Breakfast
- B Drizzle
- C The weekend
- D Easter

37
On a map, what do 'contour' lines represent?

- A Length
- B Width
- C Height
- D Golf courses

38
Which country has the world's biggest population?

- A USA
- B Russia
- C China
- D India

39
Which country is known as the 'Emerald Isle'?

- A Jersey
- B Iceland
- C Greenland
- D Ireland

40
What did Peter Pan leave behind in the Darling nursery?

- A His shadow
- B His childhood
- C His innocence
- D His wallet

answers turn to page 56

41

Who lifted the World Cup as England captain in 1966?

- A Bobby Charlton
- B Geoff Hurst
- C Jack Charlton
- D Bobby Moore

42

Which sign of the zodiac is represented by a crab?

- A Pisces
- B Cancer
- C Libra
- D Capricorn

43

What is canasta?

- A A tropical disease
- B Indian dance music
- C A card game
- D A seasonal shrub

44

What actually happens during a solar eclipse?

- A The Sun blocks the Moon
- B The Moon blocks the Sun
- C The Earth blocks the Sun
- D The Sun blocks the Earth

45

What is a dromedary?

- A An ant hill
- B A sailing vessel
- C A camel
- D A skincare specialist

46

Which train station gave its name to a fictional character?

- A Paddington
- B Victoria
- C Waterloo
- D Marylebone

47

Who owns the Canary Islands?

- A Morocco
- B Portugal
- C Britain
- D Spain

48

What is Sheffield most famous for producing?

- A Coal
- B Clothes
- C Iron
- D Steel

answers

turn to page 56

take two

turn to page 56

49
What fraction of an iceberg can be seen above the water?

- ◆ A A third
- ◆ B A quarter
- ◆ C A seventh
- ◆ D A ninth

50
The island of Alcatraz lies in the bay of which US city?

- ◆ A New York
- ◆ B Los Angeles
- ◆ C Miami
- ◆ D San Francisco

51
Where is it thought the Great Fire of London started?

- ◆ A A butcher's
- ◆ B A baker's
- ◆ C A candlestickmaker's
- ◆ D The fire station

52
What does 'poly' mean?

- ◆ A Many
- ◆ B None
- ◆ C Few
- ◆ D Pretty

53
Where is the Dow Jones stock exchange?

- ◆ A Tokyo
- ◆ B Frankfurt
- ◆ C London
- ◆ D New York

54
What is halitosis?

- ◆ A Dandruff
- ◆ B Flaky skin
- ◆ C Bad breath
- ◆ D Runny nose

55
What is the highest rank in the Navy?

- ◆ A Captain
- ◆ B Admiral
- ◆ C General
- ◆ D First Mate

56
Where was a wooden horse used as a military device?

- ◆ A York
- ◆ B Troy
- ◆ C Marathon
- ◆ D Pantomime

turn to page 56

57
At which film festival is the Palmes d'or awarded?

- A Berlin
- B Cannes
- C Sundance
- D Prague

58
What does a megalomaniac thirst for?

- A Power
- B Money
- C Glory
- D Water

59
Where are the smallest bones in the human body?

- A The foot
- B The hand
- C The ear
- D The back

60
What is the Japanese drink sake made from?

- A Potatoes
- B Noodles
- C Apples
- D Rice

61
Mocha is a variety of which drink?

- A Whisky
- B Coffee
- C Milk
- D Beer

62
What term describes Italian-made western films?

- A Ravioli
- B Pizza
- C Spaghetti
- D Pasta

63
On which continent do Inuits predominantly live?

- A Asia
- B North America
- C Antarctica
- D Australasia

64
What kind of languages are Cobol and Pascal?

- A Ancient languages
- B Martian languages
- C Animal languages
- D Computer languages

answers

turn to page 56

53

65
Which crop covers 1/5 of France's agricultural land?

- A Wheat
- B Grapes
- C Maize
- D Onions

66
Which US state has the longest border with Canada?

- A Illinois
- B Washington
- C Alaska
- D North Dakota

67
Who would perform a grande jêté?

- A An ice-skater
- B A ballet dancer
- C A trapeze artist
- D A synchronised swimmer

68
In which section of the orchestra would you find a glockenspiel?

- A Brass
- B Percussion
- C String
- D Woodwind

69
What did Clarence Birdseye invent?

- A Caviar
- B Frozen food
- C Fish paste
- D False beards

70
What does a frugivore eat?

- A Meat
- B Vegetables
- C Nuts
- D Fruit

71
What is the natural force pulling objects towards the Earth?

- A Gravity
- B Weight
- C Wind
- D Magnetism

72
What is measured on the Beaufort Scale?

- A Earthquakes
- B Wind
- C Breath
- D Mental agility

answers
turn to page 56

turn to page 56

73
What is the hardest substance in the human body?

- A Tooth enamel
- B Bone
- C Nail
- D Hair

74
With which musical style is Bob Marley associated?

- A Blues
- B Easy listening
- C Reggae
- D Dance

75
When do the Wimbledon Tennis Championships begin?

- A May
- B June
- C July
- D August

76
With which type of food are prawn crackers often served?

- A Italian
- B Mexican
- C Indian
- D Chinese

77
If you have your food 'al fresco', how do you eat it?

- A On your lap
- B With your fingers
- C Cold
- D Outdoors

78
Which mineral is important in maintaining strong teeth?

- A Iron
- B Calcium
- C Sodium
- D Potassium

79
The Sphinx had the body of which animal?

- A Lioness
- B Tiger
- C Horse
- D Asp

80
What is the control centre of a cell called?

- A Membrane
- B Cytoplasm
- C Nucleus
- D Pentagon

answers

turn to page 56

take two

Check your options to the questions below

answers

level
five

5

take two

turn to page 68

01
In 'The Simpsons', who owns the nuclear power plant?

- A Homer Simpson
- B Montgomery Burns
- C Seymour Skinner
- D Ned Flanders

02
How many chambers does the human heart have?

- A Two
- B Three
- C Four
- D Six

03
Who wrote about Phileas Fogg's eighty day world voyage?

- A Jonathan Swift
- B Daniel Defoe
- C Jules Verne
- D Lewis Carroll

04
What does the term 'equine' relate to?

- A Water
- B Ecuador
- C Painting
- D Horses

05
Who has a secretary called Miss Moneypenny?

- A M
- B Q
- C James Bond
- D 006

06
In which country was Ricky Martin born?

- A USA
- B Mexico
- C Costa Rica
- D Puerto Rico

07
What is an aperitif?

- A A starter
- B A pudding
- C A drink
- D A side dish

08
What is the area between the sea and a river called?

- A An inlet
- B An estuary
- C A reservoir
- D A strait

answers
turn to page 68

take **e** two

turn to page 68

09
What is the name of the international police force?

- A Interpol
- B CIA
- C Flying Squad
- D SWAT

10
Which is the biggest ocean?

- A Atlantic
- B Arctic
- C Indian
- D Pacific

11
Which film won a record-equalling 11 Oscars in 1997?

- A 'Shakespeare In Love'
- B 'Saving Private Ryan'
- C 'As Good as it Gets'
- D 'Titanic'

12
What does 0.25 X 0.25 equal?

- A Three-quarters
- B Half
- C An eighth
- D A sixteenth

13
Which famous building stands in Threadneedle Street?

- A Big Ben
- B The Bank of England
- C The Albert Hall
- D St. Paul's Cathedral

14
Which country has the drachma as its unit of currency?

- A Greece
- B Algeria
- C Romania
- D Saudi Arabia

15
Who famously rode naked through the streets of Coventry?

- A Boadicea
- B Lady Godiva
- C Margaret Thatcher
- D Gordon Strachan

16
Where is a sword kept?

- A A sheath
- B A spleen
- C A scabbard
- D A gourd

answers

turn to page 68

turn to page 68

17
Which is England's second city?

- ◆A Manchester
- ◆B Birmingham
- ◆C Oxford
- ◆D Bristol

18
Which acid is found in lemon juice?

- ◆A Hydrochloric acid
- ◆B Citric acid
- ◆C Sulphuric acid
- ◆D Acetic acid

19
If the height of a cube is 4 metres, what is its volume?

- ◆A 16 m³
- ◆B 24 m³
- ◆C 64 m³
- ◆D 96 m³

20
Who was Charles II's famous mistress?

- ◆A Marie Antoinette
- ◆B Jane Howard
- ◆C Nell Gwynn
- ◆D Lady Jane Grey

21
Who used to be known as PJ and Duncan?

- ◆A Morecombe and Wise
- ◆B Ant and Dec
- ◆C Reeves and Mortimer
- ◆D Phats and Small

22
The prune is a dried form of which fruit?

- ◆A Damson
- ◆B Plum
- ◆C Grape
- ◆D Apricot

23
Celluloid is an alternative name for which entertainment medium?

- ◆A Mime
- ◆B Cinema
- ◆C Cartoons
- ◆D Modern art

24
What was Woodstock?

- ◆A A music festival
- ◆B A political movement
- ◆C A naturist reserve
- ◆D A financial scandal

turn to page 68

 turn to page 68

25

The dish teryaki comes from which country?

- ◆A Korea
- ◆B China
- ◆C Japan
- ◆D Egypt

26

Which edible nut is shaped like a kidney?

- ◆A Pistachio
- ◆B Peanut
- ◆C Brazil
- ◆D Cashew

27

What is an overused phrase that has lost its impact called?

- ◆A Passé
- ◆B An old hat
- ◆C A cliché
- ◆D A soundbite

28

What is a palomino?

- ◆A A horse
- ◆B An American tribesman
- ◆C A cardigan
- ◆D A weapon

29

Where was the book 'Lord of the Flies' set?

- ◆A A desert island
- ◆B A stately home
- ◆C A hospital
- ◆D A skyscraper

30

What was the quadrant invented to assist?

- ◆A Space travel
- ◆B Navigation
- ◆C Shopping
- ◆D Building

31

Who shared a Nobel prize for her work in radioactivity?

- ◆A Emmeline Pankhurst
- ◆B Marie Curie
- ◆C Mother Teresa
- ◆D Indira Gandhi

32

In which part of the orchestra would you find a cor anglais?

- ◆A Woodwind
- ◆B String
- ◆C Audience
- ◆D Percussion

turn to page 68

61

33

What did Isaac Singer invent?

- A The microphone
- B The sewing machine
- C The kettle
- D The vacuum cleaner

34

In which sport is 'tacking' a recognised procedure?

- A Sailing
- B Sewing
- C Surfing
- D Skiing

35

In which job was press-ganging a common technique?

- A Sailor
- B Soldier
- C Miner
- D Journalist

36

How are haricot beans better known?

- A Runner beans
- B Baked beans
- C Kidney beans
- D Green beans

37

Which type of tree is the tallest in the world?

- A American pine
- B Dutch elm
- C Redwood
- D Bonsai

38

What was James Herriott's profession?

- A Doctor
- B Lawyer
- C Hunter
- D Vet

39

Who is the Greek goddess of victory?

- A Athena
- B Nike
- C Victoris
- D Thea

40

How many players are there in a basketball team?

- A Six
- B Seven
- C Five
- D Eight

turn to page 68

41

In the Bible, who pulled the temple down on top of himself?

- A Jesus
- B Cain
- C Moses
- D Samson

42

What does an archer carry his arrows in?

- A A gourd
- B A quiver
- C A plume
- D A trestle

43

Who wrote 'Robinson Crusoe'?

- A Robert Louis Stevenson
- B Samuel Johnson
- C Jonathan Swift
- D Daniel Defoe

44

Who is Ernst Stavro Blofeld's arch enemy?

- A Sherlock Holmes
- B Buck Rogers
- C Indiana Jones
- D James Bond

45

What do amateur boxers wear that professionals don't?

- A Vests
- B Headguards
- C Socks
- D Gumshields

46

'Et tu, Brute?' are thought to be whose last words?

- A Socrates
- B Julius Caesar
- C Nero
- D Alexander the Great

47

Where are British kings and queens crowned?

- A Westminster Abbey
- B St. Paul's Cathedral
- C Buckingham Palace
- D The Houses of Parliament

48

What does the Latin word 'gratis' mean?

- A Extra
- B True
- C Please
- D Free

turn to page 68

63

49
Which country does a rioja wine come from?

- A Spain
- B Italy
- C France
- D Portugal

50
In which season is hail most likely to occur?

- A Spring
- B Summer
- C Autumn
- D Winter

51
What makes up the main diet of a basking shark?

- A Fish
- B Humans
- C Seals
- D Plankton

52
What is made from almonds, sugar and eggs?

- A Icing sugar
- B Marzipan
- C Turkish Delight
- D Meringue

53
How did Dick Turpin make his name?

- A As a soldier
- B As a politician
- C As a highwayman
- D As a bank robber

54
What do 574 millilitres represent?

- A A pint
- B A pitcher
- C A thirst
- D A quart

55
Which language did the Vikings speak?

- A Scandinavian
- B Danish
- C Swedish
- D Norse

56
In which county is Gatwick Airport?

- A Hampshire
- B Surrey
- C Berkshire
- D West Sussex

57

In which profession do you need an equity card?

- A Banking
- B Horse training
- C Acting
- D Law

58

What name is given to payments made after a divorce?

- A Alimony
- B Dividends
- C Settlements
- D Acrimony

59

What is a felon?

- A A claw
- B A criminal
- C A barrel
- D A gaslight

60

Where in the body is your femur?

- A Shin
- B Thigh
- C Forearm
- D Foot

61

What is Peter Roget famous for devising?

- A Rubik's cube
- B The thesaurus
- C Monopoly
- D The internet

62

In which game is 'en passant' a recognised technique?

- A Chess
- B Draughts
- C Mah-jong
- D Bridge

63

What does the last A of NASA stand for?

- A Association
- B Astronaut
- C Administration
- D Airborne

64

What is a tsunami?

- A A raw-fish dish
- B A samurai sword
- C A tidal wave
- D A Tokyo taxi

 answers

turn to   page 68

 65

65
Who designed St. Paul's Cathedral?

- A Frank Lloyd-Wright
- B Sir Christopher Wren
- C Gaudi
- D Sir Thomas More

66
What is the surface of a spaceshuttle coated with?

- A Tiles
- B Paint
- C Grease
- D Wax

67
What is glass made from?

- A Carbon fibre
- B Crystallised rock
- C Sand
- D Perspex

68
From which country do Volvo cars originate?

- A Germany
- B Netherlands
- C Sweden
- D Denmark

69
Which BBC radio channel is centred around classical music?

- A Two
- B Three
- C Four
- D Five

70
If you enter a 'boulangerie', what are you likely to be buying?

- A Meat
- B Fruit
- C Lingerie
- D Bread

71
Who was the leader of Russia's 1917 revolution?

- A Lenin
- B Stalin
- C Trotsky
- D Merlin

72
Which fashion designer was known as 'Coco'?

- A Saint-Laurent
- B Dior
- C Chanel
- D Leshark

turn to ● page 68

73
What kind of painter was Claude Monet?

- A Renaissance
- B Impressionist
- C Modernist
- D Grafitti

74
Which type of fish becomes a kipper?

- A Mackerel
- B Cod
- C Roach
- D Herring

75
What does a seismologist study?

- A Avalanches
- B Earthquakes
- C Floods
- D Volcanoes

76
Which everyday device contains a cathode ray tube?

- A Telephone
- B Radio
- C Television
- D Car

77
What is the Fosbury Flop technique used in?

- A Wrestling
- B Self-defence
- C Share dealing
- D High-jumping

78
With which country was Britain at war over the Falklands?

- A Argentina
- B France
- C Indonesia
- D South Africa

79
Which suit might be worn with a cummerbund?

- A Business suit
- B Evening suit
- C Morning suit
- D Birthday suit

80
How frequently does a quindecennial event take place?

- A Every fifteen years
- B Every twenty-five years
- C Every five years
- D Every fifty years

answers

turn to page 68

page 58	page 59	page 60	page 61	page 62
• 01 BC	• 09 AB	• 17 AB	• 25 BC	• 33 BD
• 02 AC	• 10 AD	• 18 BD	• 26 CD	• 34 AD
• 03 CD	• 11 AD	• 19 BC	• 27 AC	• 35 AC
• 04 AD	• 12 CD	• 20 AC	• 28 AB	• 36 AB
• 05 AC	• 13 CD	• 21 BC	• 29 AC	• 37 AC
• 06 BD	• 14 AC	• 22 AB	• 30 BD	• 38 AD
• 07 AC	• 15 AB	• 23 BC	• 31 AB	• 39 AB
• 08 AB	• 16 AC	• 24 AD	• 32 AB	• 40 BC

page 63	page 64	page 65	page 66	page 67
• 41 BD	• 49 AD	• 57 BC	• 65 BD	• 73 AB
• 42 BD	• 50 BC	• 58 AC	• 66 AD	• 74 AD
• 43 CD	• 51 AD	• 59 AB	• 67 AC	• 75 AB
• 44 AD	• 52 BC	• 60 BC	• 68 AC	• 76 CD
• 45 AC	• 53 AC	• 61 BD	• 69 AB	• 77 AD
• 46 BC	• 54 AD	• 62 AD	• 70 AD	• 78 AB
• 47 AB	• 55 BD	• 63 AC	• 71 AB	• 79 BC
• 48 AD	• 56 BD	• 64 BC	• 72 AC	• 80 AC

answers

page 58	page 59	page 60	page 61	page 62
• 01 B	• 09 A	• 17 B	• 25 C	• 33 B
• 02 C	• 10 D	• 18 B	• 26 D	• 34 A
• 03 C	• 11 D	• 19 C	• 27 C	• 35 A
• 04 D	• 12 D	• 20 C	• 28 A	• 36 B
• 05 A	• 13 B	• 21 B	• 29 A	• 37 C
• 06 D	• 14 A	• 22 B	• 30 B	• 38 D
• 07 C	• 15 B	• 23 B	• 31 B	• 39 B
• 08 B	• 16 C	• 24 A	• 32 A	• 40 C

page 63	page 64	page 65	page 66	page 67
• 41 D	• 49 A	• 57 C	• 65 B	• 73 B
• 42 B	• 50 B	• 58 A	• 66 A	• 74 D
• 43 A	• 51 D	• 59 B	• 67 C	• 75 B
• 44 D	• 52 B	• 60 B	• 68 C	• 76 C
• 45 A	• 53 C	• 61 B	• 69 B	• 77 D
• 46 B	• 54 A	• 62 A	• 70 D	• 78 A
• 47 A	• 55 D	• 63 C	• 71 A	• 79 B
• 48 D	• 56 D	• 64 C	• 72 C	• 80 A

level
six

take two

turn to page 80

01
Where would you get a baccalaureat?

- A In prison
- B At school
- C In hospital
- D In a restaurant

02
What is the correct term for lockjaw?

- A Tetanus
- B Typhoid
- C Rubella
- D Flu

03
Who won the Battle of Agincourt?

- A France
- B Spain
- C Germany
- D England

04
What is a chippie's official job description?

- A Electrician
- B Carpenter
- C Plumber
- D Painter

05
Where does a croupier work?

- A A bank
- B A casino
- C A restaurant
- D A hotel

06
Which TV programme does Jeremy Paxman often present?

- A Panorama
- B Channel Four News
- C Newsnight
- D Question Time

07
To whom did the Australian government apologise in 1999?

- A The Maoris
- B The Aborigines
- C The Kiwis
- D The English

08
What colour chip describes a safe company to invest in?

- A Black
- B Gold
- C Blue
- D White

 answers

 turn to page 80

turn to page 80

09

In which US state is Pearl Harbour?

- A California
- B Connecticut
- C Hawaii
- D New York State

10

What does augment mean?

- A Increase
- B Help
- C Destroy
- D Display

11

Who had the UK's millennium No. 1 single?

- A Cliff Richard
- B Westlife
- C S-Club Seven
- D Boyzone

12

Who discovered the Hawaiian Islands?

- A Ferdinand Magellan
- B James Cook
- C Christopher Columbus
- D Vasco da Gama

13

Where is Cowes Week spent?

- A Plymouth
- B Jersey
- C Southampton
- D The Isle of Wight

14

Which island boasts a collection of gigantic stone statues?

- A Christmas Island
- B Easter Island
- C Summer Island
- D New Year Island

15

Who was involved in a scandal with Monica Lewinsky?

- A Boris Yeltsin
- B Bill Clinton
- C Jacques Chirac
- D Tony Blair

16

Which substance has types called igneous and sedimentary?

- A Wood
- B Sand
- C Rock
- D Ice

turn to page 80

take two

turn to page 80

17
Which sport is played on a diamond?

- A US football
- B Baseball
- C Polo
- D Australian Rules

18
What type of fashion statement is 'a mullet'?

- A A hat
- B A shirt pattern
- C A haircut
- D A watch

19
Who declared: 'I have a dream'?

- A Malcolm X
- B Martin Luther King
- C Mahatma Ghandi
- D Nelson Mandela

20
What kind of animal is a water rat?

- A Otter
- B Vole
- C Beaver
- D Gerbil

21
Which island is disputed by Greece and Turkey?

- A Cyprus
- B Zante
- C Rhodes
- D Corfu

22
Who was Princess Diana's tribute song first written for?

- A Florence Nightingale
- B Marilyn Monroe
- C Mother Teresa
- D Joan of Arc

23
Which Beatle's daughter is a famous fashion designer?

- A John Lennon
- B Paul McCartney
- C Ringo Starr
- D George Harrison

24
What does the National Trust look after?

- A Money
- B Fossils
- C People
- D Land

answers

turn to page 80

25

What was Brazil named after?

- A A mountain
- B A river
- C A nut tree
- D A football team

26

Who were the main participants in the 'Cold War'?

- A Germany and Britain
- B USA and USSR
- C Germany and USSR
- D Iceland and Finland

27

On which continent did coffee originate?

- A Europe
- B Asia
- C Africa
- D South America

28

What is the lowest prime number?

- A One
- B Three
- C Seven
- D Eleven

29

On which surface is the French tennis Open played?

- A Grass
- B Clay
- C Carpet
- D Cement

30

In which country is the Serengeti?

- A Zimbabwe
- B Kenya
- C The Sudan
- D South Africa

31

What is India's Taj Mahal constructed from?

- A Ivory
- B Marble
- C Sandstone
- D Papier-mâché

32

Which 20th-century dictator was known as Il Duce?

- A Hitler
- B Mussolini
- C Stalin
- D Franco

answers

turn to **w** page 80

73

take two

turn to page 80

33
What do 1,024 bytes make?

- A A gigabyte
- B A kilobyte
- C A megabyte
- D A takeabite

34
The Dalai Lama is the Spiritual leader of which country?

- A Tibet
- B Nepal
- C China
- D Hong Kong

35
France, Spain, Britain, and Israel were all part of which empire?

- A Roman
- B Ottoman
- C Egyptian
- D American

36
In which city could you visit the Parthenon?

- A Cairo
- B Athens
- C Rome
- D Manchester

37
What is myopia more commonly known as?

- A Hayfever
- B Baldness
- C Forgetfulness
- D Short sight

38
What is distinctive about 'gazpacho' soup?

- A It's served in a glass
- B It's served as a dessert
- C It's served cold
- D It's served on a plate

39
Which country is represented by the letter 'D' on a car?

- A Germany
- B Dominican Republic
- C Denmark
- D Dubai

40
On which continent did the Incas live?

- A Africa
- B South America
- C Europe
- D Asia

answers

turn to page 80

turn to page 80

41

Who is reputed to be the wealthiest man in the world?

- A The Sultan of Brunei
- B Rupert Murdoch
- C Bill Gates
- D Richard Branson

42

How many decathlon events involve throwing?

- A One
- B Two
- C Three
- D Four

43

How many degrees are there inside a triangle?

- A 90°
- B 180°
- C 360°
- D 270°

44

Who wrote 'Pride and Prejudice'?

- A Jane Austen
- B T. S. Eliot
- C Emily Brontë
- D Mary Shelley

45

What is the profession of the comic book character Tintin?

- A Explorer
- B Detective
- C Spy
- D Reporter

46

Which type of bird lives in the Tower of London?

- A Blackbirds
- B Crows
- C Ravens
- D Kestrels

47

What bodily function occurs in the alimentary canal?

- A Excretion
- B Digestion
- C Respiration
- D Reproduction

48

In which country did Lego originate?

- A Denmark
- B Germany
- C Italy
- D Sweden

turn to page 80

turn to   page 80

49
What nationality was Ludwig Van Beethoven?

- A German
- B Swiss
- C Austrian
- D French

50
Which wood was mainly used in Chippendale furniture?

- A Oak
- B Pine
- C Mahogany
- D Balsa

51
Which city is most at risk from the San Andreas Fault?

- A San Francisco
- B Mexico City
- C Istanbul
- D Santiago

52
Which is Britain's highest mountain?

- A Scafell Pike
- B Snowdon
- C Box Hill
- D Ben Nevis

53
Veal is obtained from which animal?

- A Rabbit
- B Deer
- C Calf
- D Goat

54
In which month of the year is Britain's longest day?

- A May
- B June
- C July
- D August

55
What is the capital of Iraq?

- A Tehran
- B Kuwait City
- C Baghdad
- D Tripoli

56
Who is a self-confessed member of the 'West Staines Massive'?

- A Mark Morrison
- B Ali G
- C Snoop Dogg
- D Vanilla Ice

answers

turn to   page 80

57

Dartmoor is in which English county?

- A Somerset
- B Gloucestershire
- C Devon
- D Cornwall

58

Which bird is the fastest runner in the world?

- A Warbler
- B Emu
- C Pelican
- D Ostrich

59

Which country is goulash associated with?

- A Germany
- B Turkey
- C Hungary
- D Romania

60

What draws thousands to Glastonbury every year?

- A A film festival
- B A music festival
- C A car show
- D A boat show

61

What does the word recuperate mean?

- A To react
- B To remember
- C To reduce
- D To recover

62

Which is Britain's longest river?

- A Thames
- B Severn
- C Clyde
- D Trent

63

Of what was Thor the Viking god?

- A Thunder
- B War
- C Wisdom
- D Culture

64

Who was known as the Mad Monk?

- A Quasimodo
- B Nostradamus
- C Rasputin
- D Friar Tuck

65

What is the name of a jockey's outfit?

- A Colours
- B Slips
- C Silks
- D Suits

66

What would you find in an apiary?

- A Primates
- B Bees
- C Ants
- D Tropical plants

67

A car travels 320 miles in 5 hours. What's its average speed?

- A 60 mph
- B 64 mph
- C 68 mph
- D 72 mph

68

In which decade did Britain first see colour television?

- A 1940s
- B 1950s
- C 1960s
- D 1970s

69

In which sport can the attacking side earn a penalty corner?

- A Field hockey
- B Curling
- C Ice hockey
- D Hurling

70

What do the French refer to as La Manche?

- A Easter
- B Midnight
- C Wales
- D The English Channel

71

How many times the speed of sound is Mach 2?

- A Half
- B Twice
- C Four
- D Ten

72

In which performing art was Margot Fonteyn famous?

- A Opera
- B Theatre
- C Ballet
- D Classical music

turn to page 80

73

From which country does the bossa nova dance originate?

- A Brazil
- B Jamaica
- C Fiji
- D Samoa

74

What does the disease impetigo affect?

- A Eyes
- B Skin
- C Hair
- D Throat

75

From which country do Saxons mainly originate?

- A Britain
- B Sweden
- C Germany
- D France

76

Which colour is used to denote the easiest ski runs?

- A Blue
- B Black
- C Red
- D Green

77

If a cat is feline, what is a sheep?

- A Canine
- B Bovine
- C Ovine
- D Equine

78

What do the Japanese call Japan?

- A Takechi
- B Nippon
- C Hirohito
- D Rising Sun

79

Poseidon and Neptune were the Greek and Roman gods of what?

- A The moon
- B The sun
- C The land
- D The sea

80

What is a kleptomaniac addicted to?

- A Stealing
- B Gambling
- C Lying
- D Danger

 answers turn to page 80

take two

Check your options to the questions below

page 70		page 71		page 72		page 73		page 74	
◆ 01	BD	◆ 09	AC	◆ 17	BD	◆ 25	BC	◆ 33	AC
◆ 02	AC	◆ 10	AB	◆ 18	AC	◆ 26	AB	◆ 34	AB
◆ 03	AD	◆ 11	AC	◆ 19	BD	◆ 27	BD	◆ 35	AC
◆ 04	AB	◆ 12	BC	◆ 20	AB	◆ 28	AC	◆ 36	BC
◆ 05	AB	◆ 13	BD	◆ 21	AD	◆ 29	BD	◆ 37	BD
◆ 06	AC	◆ 14	BC	◆ 22	BC	◆ 30	AB	◆ 38	BC
◆ 07	AB	◆ 15	AB	◆ 23	AB	◆ 31	AB	◆ 39	AC
◆ 08	BC	◆ 16	CD	◆ 24	AD	◆ 32	BD	◆ 40	BD

page 75		page 76		page 77		page 78		page 79	
◆ 41	AC	◆ 49	AC	◆ 57	CD	◆ 65	AC	◆ 73	AB
◆ 42	BC	◆ 50	AC	◆ 58	BD	◆ 66	BC	◆ 74	AB
◆ 43	BC	◆ 51	AD	◆ 59	CD	◆ 67	BC	◆ 75	AC
◆ 44	AB	◆ 52	BD	◆ 60	AB	◆ 68	BC	◆ 76	AD
◆ 45	BD	◆ 53	BC	◆ 61	BD	◆ 69	AD	◆ 77	BC
◆ 46	BC	◆ 54	BC	◆ 62	BC	◆ 70	BD	◆ 78	AB
◆ 47	AB	◆ 55	AC	◆ 63	AB	◆ 71	BC	◆ 79	AD
◆ 48	AD	◆ 56	AB	◆ 64	BC	◆ 72	AC	◆ 80	AC

answers

page 70		page 71		page 72		page 73		page 74	
◆ 01	B	◆ 09	C	◆ 17	B	◆ 25	C	◆ 33	C
◆ 02	A	◆ 10	A	◆ 18	C	◆ 26	B	◆ 34	A
◆ 03	D	◆ 11	A	◆ 19	B	◆ 27	D	◆ 35	A
◆ 04	B	◆ 12	B	◆ 20	B	◆ 28	A	◆ 36	B
◆ 05	B	◆ 13	D	◆ 21	A	◆ 29	B	◆ 37	D
◆ 06	C	◆ 14	B	◆ 22	B	◆ 30	B	◆ 38	C
◆ 07	B	◆ 15	B	◆ 23	B	◆ 31	B	◆ 39	A
◆ 08	C	◆ 16	C	◆ 24	D	◆ 32	B	◆ 40	B

page 75		page 76		page 77		page 78		page 79	
◆ 41	C	◆ 49	A	◆ 57	C	◆ 65	C	◆ 73	A
◆ 42	C	◆ 50	C	◆ 58	B	◆ 66	B	◆ 74	B
◆ 43	B	◆ 51	A	◆ 59	C	◆ 67	B	◆ 75	C
◆ 44	A	◆ 52	D	◆ 60	B	◆ 68	C	◆ 76	D
◆ 45	D	◆ 53	C	◆ 61	D	◆ 69	A	◆ 77	C
◆ 46	C	◆ 54	B	◆ 62	B	◆ 70	D	◆ 78	B
◆ 47	B	◆ 55	C	◆ 63	A	◆ 71	B	◆ 79	D
◆ 48	A	◆ 56	B	◆ 64	C	◆ 72	C	◆ 80	A

level
seven

7

01
Where would you find a coxswain?

- A In a pub
- B In a boat
- C In a museum
- D In a church

02
Who was the Roman god of love?

- A Cupid
- B Venus
- C Mercury
- D Valentine

03
What is the back of a boat called?

- A Bow
- B Stern
- C Port
- D Starboard

04
Which country was called Hibernia in Latin?

- A England
- B Wales
- C Scotland
- D Ireland

05
Which country did Iraq invade in 1990 to start the Gulf War?

- A Iran
- B Afghanistan
- C Israel
- D Kuwait

06
Who fought in the Wars of the Roses?

- A North and South
- B Roundheads and Cavaliers
- C Yorkists and Lancastrians
- D Unionists and Republicans

07
What is sodium chloride more commonly known as?

- A Sugar
- B Water
- C Flour
- D Salt

08
Which is the longest river in the world?

- A Amazon
- B Mississippi
- C Ganges
- D Mole

09
Which town gave its name to sherry?

- A Cheruy, France
- B Sheringham, England
- C Jerez, Spain
- D Sherridon, Canada

10
What does a red flag mean to a Formula One racing driver?

- A Disqualification
- B Stop racing
- C Mechanical problems
- D You're speeding

11
What name is given to hot air rising?

- A Convection
- B Conduction
- C Refraction
- D Infection

12
What do Kelvins measure?

- A Acceleration
- B Pressure
- C Temperature
- D Depth

13
How many seas are named after colours?

- A Two
- B Three
- C Four
- D Five

14
What do you keep in a butt?

- A Gunpowder
- B Food
- C Rubbish
- D Water

15
What is didactics?

- A Nursing
- B Arithmetic
- C Teaching
- D Grammar

16
How is lumbago more commonly known?

- A Headache
- B Backache
- C Indigestion
- D Heartburn

 answers

turn to page 92

83

17
Where did the 1999 Polar lander mission fail to land?

- A Mars
- B Jupiter
- C Uranus
- D Pluto

18
What does the term fiscal relate to?

- A Money
- B The sea
- C Travel
- D The muscles

19
Over which European state did Serbia go to war in 1999?

- A Hungary
- B Kosovo
- C Romania
- D Poland

20
What does the word doner mean, in doner kebab?

- A Lamb
- B Rotating
- C Grease
- D Shavings

21
Which part of the body does gingivitis effect?

- A Eyes
- B Teeth
- C Gums
- D Nostrils

22
As king, Prince William would be known by which number?

- A III
- B IV
- C V
- D VI

23
Who writes and stars in the Austin Powers films?

- A Ben Stiller
- B Adam Sandler
- C Mike Myers
- D Kevin Smith

24
How many people are needed to carry a sedan chair?

- A None
- B Two
- C Four
- D Six

25

Which battle did England and Scotland fight in 1314?

- ◆A Culloden
- ◆B Bannockburn
- ◆C Braveheart
- ◆D Glasgow

26

What does the A in VAT stand for?

- ◆A Added
- ◆B Additional
- ◆C Allied
- ◆D Appropriate

27

What does GM stand for in relation to food?

- ◆A Genetically Modulated
- ◆B Genetically Moderated
- ◆C Genetically Modified
- ◆D Genetically Manufactured

28

Which land animal lives longer than any other?

- ◆A Human
- ◆B Elephant
- ◆C Tortoise
- ◆D Ostrich

29

If a car is decribed as a V8, what does it have 8 of?

- ◆A Carburettors
- ◆B Axles
- ◆C Gears
- ◆D Cylinders

30

What is a group of owls called?

- ◆A A senate
- ◆B A forum
- ◆C A parliament
- ◆D A house of commons

31

In which country did lawn tennis originate?

- ◆A India
- ◆B France
- ◆C England
- ◆D Sweden

32

What name is given to a tailored suit?

- ◆A Specified
- ◆B Bespoke
- ◆C Vented
- ◆D Off the peg

answers

turn to page 92

take two

turn to page 92

33
Which is the most frequently used word in English?

- A And
- B The
- C It
- D A

34
In which sport is the Ryder Cup contested?

- A Golf
- B Sailing
- C Tennis
- D Horse racing

35
On which racecourse is the Grand National run?

- A Epsom
- B Newmarket
- C Goodwood
- D Aintree

36
What is the medical term for the voicebox?

- A Larynx
- B Trachea
- C Windpipe
- D Oesophagus

37
Which book is Kenneth Grahame famous for writing?

- A 'The Jungle Book'
- B 'Swallows and Amazons'
- C 'Wind in the Willows'
- D 'Alice in Wonderland'

38
What is the name of Sicily's major volcano?

- A Vesuvius
- B Etna
- C Krakatoa
- D Stromboli

39
How would you address an ambassador?

- A Your majesty
- B Your honour
- C Your excellency
- D Sir

40
How long is the coastline of California?

- A 73 miles
- B 234 miles
- C 1,350 miles
- D 4,500 miles

turn to page 92

41
What did William Caxton introduce to England?

- A Printing
- B Two-way radio
- C Morse code
- D Telephone

42
What would you be suffering from if you had mal au coeur?

- A Heartache
- B Stomach ache
- C Travel sickness
- D Home sickness

43
Which war began in 1642?

- A One Hundred Years War
- B Wars of the Roses
- C English Civil War
- D American Civil War

44
What does the word forte mean, in music?

- A Strongly
- B Loudly
- C Quickly
- D Slowly

45
In which month of the year is Hogmanay celebrated?

- A November
- B December
- C January
- D February

46
Who wrote 'Frankenstein'?

- A Daniel Defoe
- B Bram Stoker
- C Thomas Hardy
- D Mary Shelley

47
Which is the lowest rank in the British nobility?

- A Baron
- B Earl
- C Duke
- D Viscount

48
Who fell in love with his own reflection?

- A Pericles
- B Theolonius
- C Narcissus
- D Beckham

answers turn to page 92

turn to page 92

49

In which of the arts is Placido Domingo a famous name?

- A Cinema
- B Theatre
- C Opera
- D Art

50

What does the M of MCC stand for?

- A Maida Vale
- B Marylebone
- C Middlesex
- D Manchester

51

In which city did Anne Frank write her famous diary?

- A Amsterdam
- B Berlin
- C Paris
- D Brussels

52

What family is the trout a member of?

- A Salmon
- B Tuna
- C Mackerel
- D Shark

53

Who was born Cassius Clay?

- A Nicholas Cage
- B Stevie Wonder
- C Denzel Washington
- D Mohammad Ali

54

What does a Geiger counter measure?

- A Extreme temperature
- B Nuclear radiation
- C Sound waves
- D Air moisture

55

Who is seen as the originator of psychoanalysis?

- A Clement Freud
- B Emma Freud
- C Sigmund Freud
- D Lucian Freud

56

What is the natural environment of a gerbil?

- A Mountain
- B Forest
- C City
- D Desert

turn to page 92

turn to page 92

57

Prince's street is the main thoroughfare of which city?

- A Glasgow
- B Edinburgh
- C Aberdeen
- D Dundee

58

What does 'bio' mean?

- A Air
- B Organism
- C Life
- D Yoghurt

59

What is Billingsgate market famous for selling?

- A Records
- B Clothes
- C Jewellery
- D Fish

60

Cape Horn lies at the tip of which continent?

- A Africa
- B Asia
- C Antartica
- D South America

61

What is a gastronome interested in?

- A Fast cars
- B Good food
- C Classical music
- D Exotic holidays

62

Where is the Barbary apes' most famous home?

- A Gibraltar
- B Malta
- C Lanzarote
- D Madagascar

63

Which US president was previously a film star?

- A Woodrow Wilson
- B Lyndon B. Johnson
- C Franklin D. Roosevelt
- D Ronald Reagan

64

What is a fully grown gherkin called?

- A A cucumber
- B A zucchini
- C A marrow
- D A courgette

turn to page 92

take two

turn to page 92

65
What is a dhow?

- A A payment
- B A headdress
- C A boat
- D A currency

66
How many of the Seven Wonders of the World are still standing?

- A Five
- B Three
- C One
- D None

67
What is precipitation better known as?

- A Traffic
- B Anxiety
- C Rain
- D Sweat

68
In which country was the Boer War fought?

- A South Africa
- B India
- C Egypt
- D China

69
When does a liquid become a gas?

- A When it is heated
- B When it is condensed
- C When it is cooled
- D When it is drunk

70
What is the surgical name for a 'nose job'?

- A Hippoplasty
- B Eleplasty
- C Cornishplasty
- D Rhinoplasty

71
Which Derbyshire town shares its name with a type of sofa?

- A Sudbury
- B Chesterfield
- C Matlock
- D Buxton

72
In the Chinese calendar, what represents the year 2000?

- A Tiger
- B Rabbit
- C Rat
- D Dragon

answers turn to page 92

73
In which country is the state of Natal?

- A South Africa
- B Zimbabwe
- C New Zealand
- D Canada

74
What is the name of the fin that runs down the back of a fish?

- A Pectoral fin
- B Caudal fin
- C Dorsal fin
- D Pelvic fin

75
Which province of Canada is predominantly French speaking?

- A Ontario
- B Nova Scotia
- C Ottawa
- D Quebec

76
In which city did Princess Diana die?

- A London
- B New York
- C Paris
- D Rome

77
In the book 'Animal Farm', what type of animal is Napoleon?

- A A cow
- B A pig
- C A horse
- D A chicken

78
Which substance symbolises a first wedding anniversary?

- A Gold
- B Wood
- C Water
- D Paper

79
Who has the motto 'Who Dares Wins'?

- A The SAS
- B The Scouts
- C The RAF
- D The Salvation Army

80
What tree type is most often used as a Christmas tree?

- A American pine
- B Norway spruce
- C Conifer
- D Palm

answers turn to page 92

tak**e**two

Check your options to the questions below

page 82	page 83	page 84	page 85	page 86
◆ 01 BD	◆ 09 AC	◆ 17 AD	◆ 25 AB	◆ 33 BD
◆ 02 AB	◆ 10 AB	◆ 18 AB	◆ 26 AB	◆ 34 AB
◆ 03 AB	◆ 11 AB	◆ 19 BD	◆ 27 CD	◆ 35 BD
◆ 04 CD	◆ 12 BC	◆ 20 AB	◆ 28 BC	◆ 36 AD
◆ 05 AD	◆ 13 AC	◆ 21 BC	◆ 29 BD	◆ 37 AC
◆ 06 BC	◆ 14 CD	◆ 22 BC	◆ 30 AC	◆ 38 AB
◆ 07 AD	◆ 15 CD	◆ 23 AC	◆ 31 AB	◆ 39 BC
◆ 08 AB	◆ 16 BC	◆ 24 BC	◆ 32 BC	◆ 40 CD

page 87	page 88	page 89	page 90	page 91
◆ 41 AC	◆ 49 AC	◆ 57 AB	◆ 65 CD	◆ 73 AD
◆ 42 AC	◆ 50 AB	◆ 58 BC	◆ 66 BC	◆ 74 AC
◆ 43 CD	◆ 51 AD	◆ 59 CD	◆ 67 AC	◆ 75 AD
◆ 44 AB	◆ 52 AC	◆ 60 AD	◆ 68 AC	◆ 76 AC
◆ 45 BC	◆ 53 BD	◆ 61 BD	◆ 69 AB	◆ 77 BC
◆ 46 CD	◆ 54 BC	◆ 62 AC	◆ 70 BD	◆ 78 BD
◆ 47 AB	◆ 55 AC	◆ 63 AD	◆ 71 BC	◆ 79 AC
◆ 48 BC	◆ 56 AD	◆ 64 AD	◆ 72 AD	◆ 80 AB

ans**w**ers

page 82	page 83	page 84	page 85	page 86
◆ 01 B	◆ 09 C	◆ 17 A	◆ 25 B	◆ 33 B
◆ 02 A	◆ 10 B	◆ 18 A	◆ 26 A	◆ 34 A
◆ 03 B	◆ 11 A	◆ 19 B	◆ 27 C	◆ 35 D
◆ 04 C	◆ 12 C	◆ 20 B	◆ 28 C	◆ 36 A
◆ 05 D	◆ 13 C	◆ 21 C	◆ 29 D	◆ 37 C
◆ 06 C	◆ 14 D	◆ 22 C	◆ 30 C	◆ 38 B
◆ 07 D	◆ 15 C	◆ 23 C	◆ 31 B	◆ 39 C
◆ 08 A	◆ 16 B	◆ 24 B	◆ 32 B	◆ 40 C

page 87	page 88	page 89	page 90	page 91
◆ 41 A	◆ 49 C	◆ 57 B	◆ 65 C	◆ 73 A
◆ 42 C	◆ 50 B	◆ 58 C	◆ 66 C	◆ 74 C
◆ 43 C	◆ 51 A	◆ 59 D	◆ 67 C	◆ 75 D
◆ 44 B	◆ 52 A	◆ 60 D	◆ 68 A	◆ 76 C
◆ 45 B	◆ 53 D	◆ 61 B	◆ 69 A	◆ 77 B
◆ 46 C	◆ 54 B	◆ 62 A	◆ 70 D	◆ 78 D
◆ 47 A	◆ 55 C	◆ 63 D	◆ 71 B	◆ 79 A
◆ 48 C	◆ 56 D	◆ 64 A	◆ 72 D	◆ 80 B

level
eight

8

take two

turn to page 104

01

In John Wyndham's book, what are the Triffids?

- ◆A Plants
- ◆B Aliens
- ◆C Sea creatures
- ◆D Zombies

02

What does the word celestial refer to?

- ◆A Vegetables
- ◆B The sea
- ◆C The sky
- ◆D Ghosts

03

What is vivisection another word for?

- ◆A Testing on animals
- ◆B Cannibalism
- ◆C Germ warfare
- ◆D Child labour

04

What name is given to the fuel injection system in a jet engine?

- ◆A Turbo
- ◆B Booster
- ◆C Supercharge
- ◆D Afterburner

05

Which part of the body does glaucoma affect?

- ◆A The kidneys
- ◆B The eyes
- ◆C The nose
- ◆D The skin

06

Which ingredient makes popcorn pop?

- ◆A Starch
- ◆B Salt
- ◆C Water
- ◆D Semtex

07

How many quavers are there in a crotchet?

- ◆A Two
- ◆B Four
- ◆C Six
- ◆D Eight

08

In music, which word describes how high or low a note is?

- ◆A Depth
- ◆B Tone
- ◆C Pitch
- ◆D Quality

answers

turn to page 104

09
Which religion was founded by Mohammed?

* A Islam
* B Judaism
* C Buddhism
* D Sikhism

10
Which people did Genghis Khan rule over?

* A The Huns
* B The Mongols
* C The Turks
* D The Shiites

11
Who united Italy in 1879?

* A De Medici
* B Galileo
* C Garibaldi
* D Bourbon

12
Which county is described as the garden of England?

* A Shropshire
* B Dorset
* C Kent
* D Suffolk

13
What was first used at the Battle of the Somme?

* A The machine gun
* B The tank
* C The bayonet
* D The helicopter

14
What is Esperanto?

* A A dance
* B A painting style
* C A herb
* D A language

15
How long does it take the Moon to revolve around the Earth?

* A 1 day
* B 7 days
* C 28 days
* D 365 days

16
When did man first set foot on the Moon?

* A 1960
* B 1964
* C 1969
* D 1974

take two

turn to page 104

17
Which gas is the most abundant in the Earth's atmosphere?

- A Carbon Dioxide
- B Oxygen
- C Nitrogen
- D Ozone

18
Who is the patron saint of Wales?

- A Owen
- B Neil
- C David
- D Matthew

19
Who built the Rocket locomotive in 1829?

- A Robert Stephenson
- B Samuel Stephenson
- C George Stephenson
- D Juliet Stevenson

20
In which British city is Tiger Bay?

- A Glasgow
- B Cardiff
- C Bristol
- D Swansea

21
Where is a baby's fontanelle?

- A On the head
- B In the navel
- C In the mouth
- D In the nose

22
How many strings are there on a violin?

- A Three
- B Four
- C Five
- D Six

23
Which hills form the border between England and Scotland?

- A The Southern Uplands
- B The Sperrins
- C The Cairngorms
- D The Cheviots

24
How many points is a bullseye worth on a dartboard?

- A 25
- B 40
- C 50
- D 60

answers

turn to page 104

25
What was invented by cyclist John Keen in 1873?

- A Helmets
- B Brakes
- C Cycle lanes
- D Spokes

26
In Welsh, what is Wales known as?

- A Cymru
- B Galles
- C Plaid
- D Rhyll

27
What does the Munich Oktoberfest celebrate?

- A Opera
- B Beer
- C Food
- D Comedy

28
What is the hole in the centre of the eye that lets light in?

- A Cornea
- B Iris
- C Pupil
- D Retina

29
What are people who come from Tangiers, Algeria, known as?

- A Tangerians
- B Tangerites
- C Tangerines
- D Satsumas

30
Which golfer died in his aeroplane in 1999?

- A Colin Montgomerie
- B Davis Love III
- C Greg Norman
- D Payne Stewart

31
Who invented penicillin?

- A Alexander Fleming
- B Louis Pasteur
- C Edward Jenner
- D Mark Porter

32
In which area of the arts is JMW Turner a famous name?

- A Painting
- B Sculpture
- C Modern dance
- D Poetry

answers turn to page 104

97

take two

turn to ⓔ page 104

33
The island of Bali is part of which country?

- A Malaysia
- B The Philippines
- C Indonesia
- D Thailand

34
From which animal is the material cashmere obtained?

- A A sheep
- B A goat
- C A yak
- D A cow

35
In which part of a hospital would a 'caesarean' be performed?

- A Orthopaedic
- B Maternity
- C Ear, nose and throat
- D Psychiatric

36
What do carcinogens cause?

- A Fire
- B Cancer
- C Pollution
- D Tornadoes

37
Which is the largest organ in the human body?

- A The heart
- B The large Intestine
- C The skin
- D The brain

38
What does dinosaur literally mean?

- A Terrible lizard
- B Monstrous creature
- C Destructive reptile
- D Ancient beast

39
Where did Mother Teresa carry out her work with the starving?

- A Cairo
- B Calcutta
- C Karachi
- D New Delhi

40
Which animal is said to have caused the most human deaths?

- A The great white shark
- B The tiger
- C The rhinoceros
- D The cobra

answers turn to ⓦ page 104

take two

turn to page 104

41

Who was Anne Hathaway's famous husband?

- A Horatio Nelson
- B Winston Churchill
- C Laurence Olivier
- D William Shakespeare

42

If someone is described as hirsute, what are they?

- A Hairy
- B Mean
- C Well-dressed
- D Wealthy

43

What do the Italians call the city of Florence?

- A Fiorentina
- B Firenze
- C Florenzia
- D Florentine

44

In which English county is the Lake District?

- A Lancashire
- B Cleveland
- C Cumbria
- D Derbyshire

45

Where might you celebrate the Day of the Dead?

- A China
- B Peru
- C Mexico
- D Tanzania

46

Which English king abdicated his throne in 1935?

- A George VI
- B Phillip II
- C Edward VIII
- D Charles III

47

By what name is the European currency known?

- A Emu
- B Ecu
- C Euro
- D European dollar

48

What is the charity Amnesty International concerned with?

- A Homelessness
- B Human Rights
- C Memory loss
- D Pollution

answers turn to page 104

turn to page 104

49
Which team sport was originated by American Indians?

- A Rugby Union
- B Lacrosse
- C Baseball
- D Gridiron

50
What type of bird is a Rhode Island Red?

- A A chicken
- B An owl
- C An eagle
- D A duck

51
With what music is New Orleans most associated?

- A Blues
- B Jazz
- C Soul
- D Drum and bass

52
In which sport might you have to contend with moguls?

- A Windsurfing
- B Fencing
- C Skiing
- D Show jumping

53
Which profession requires trainees to get 'articles'?

- A Journalism
- B Accountancy
- C Law
- D Paper Boy

54
What was Lawrence of Arabia's nationality?

- A Arabian
- B American
- C English
- D French

55
What colour is a plug's live wire?

- A Brown
- B Blue
- C Green and yellow
- D Red

56
Which organ removes waste products from the blood?

- A The kidney
- B The small intestine
- C The heart
- D The bladder

answers turn to page 104

take two

turn to page 104

57
Which element is represented by the symbol Pb?

- ◆A Iron
- ◆B Lead
- ◆C Prombium
- ◆D Phosphorous

58
Where would you see an epitaph written?

- ◆A In a newspaper
- ◆B In a book
- ◆C On a post-it note
- ◆D On a tombstone

59
Which simple game is known in America as tick-tack-toe?

- ◆A Forty Forty
- ◆B Noughts and crosses
- ◆C Hopscotch
- ◆D Hangman

60
What type of bridge is London's Tower Bridge?

- ◆A Cantilever
- ◆B Drawbridge
- ◆C Suspension
- ◆D Arch

61
Which country did Germany invade in 1939 to ignite WWII?

- ◆A Belgium
- ◆B Russia
- ◆C Poland
- ◆D France

62
Where are your adenoids?

- ◆A The throat
- ◆B The nose
- ◆C The neck
- ◆D The chest

63
What did Paris police prefect Eugène Poubelle invent in 1883?

- ◆A The croissant
- ◆B The truncheon
- ◆C The cheque book
- ◆D The dustbin

64
What was Charles Léotard's occupation?

- ◆A Philosopher
- ◆B Trapeze artist
- ◆C Scientist
- ◆D Personal trainer

 answers

turn to page 104

turn to **e** page 104

65
Which athlete later became a Conservative politician?

- A Steve Cram
- B Sebastian Coe
- C Steve Ovett
- D Kenneth Clarke

66
What is the nucleus of a comet made of?

- A Fire
- B Rock
- C Ice
- D Gas

67
Which English king was beheaded in 1649?

- A Charles I
- B Henry VII
- C Edward VI
- D George III

68
What position did Pontius Pilate hold?

- A Governor
- B Judge
- C Priest
- D Senator

69
In which English county is Stonehenge?

- A Hampshire
- B Somerset
- C Wiltshire
- D Avon

70
At what temperature does water boil in Fahrenheit?

- A 99° F
- B 140° F
- C 194° F
- D 212° F

71
What cargo did the Cutty Sark carry?

- A Gold
- B Wine
- C Tea
- D Slaves

72
What is the highest possible poker hand, without wild cards?

- A Four of a kind
- B Full house
- C Royal flush
- D Straight

answers turn to page 104

turn to **e** page 104

73

In which US city was President John F. Kennedy assassinated?

- A Seattle
- B Dallas
- C Denver
- D Boston

74

What was Charles Richter's profession?

- A Botanist
- B Biologist
- C Geologist
- D Seismologist

75

Which Falls are on the border between Zambia and Zimbabwe?

- A Angel
- B Niagara
- C Victoria
- D Horseshoe

76

Who flew so close to the Sun that his wings melted?

- A Parallax
- B Icarus
- C Cartheus
- D Porthos

77

How many Horsemen of the Apocalypse are there?

- A Two
- B Three
- C Four
- D Five

78

Which planet is closest to the earth?

- A Venus
- B Mercury
- C Pluto
- D Mars

79

What is the name of the bony structure that protects the brain?

- A The cranium
- B The mandible
- C The cerebrum
- D The clavicle

80

Which famous building has been nicknamed the 'Peeled Orange'?

- A British Library, London
- B Pompidou Centre, Paris
- C Gaudi Catedral, Barcelona
- D Opera House, Sydney

answers turn to page 104

take two

Check your options   to the questions below

answers

take two

turn to **e** page 116

01

Casablanca is the former capital of which country?

- A Egypt
- B Algeria
- C Morocco
- D Turkey

02

The island of Jutland is part of which country?

- A Japan
- B Greenland
- C Denmark
- D The Philippines

03

What do paleontologists study?

- A Fossils
- B Dinosaurs
- C Habitats
- D Ikeas

04

Where are a horse's withers?

- A The arch of its back
- B The base of its neck
- C The centre of its chest
- D The base of its tail

05

Which type of cloud carries rain?

- A Cirrus
- B Stratus
- C Altostratus
- D Nimbus

06

Which country used to be called Ceylon?

- A India
- B Zimbabwe
- C Pakistan
- D Sri Lanka

07

Which country's cars bear the registration ES?

- A Spain
- B Estonia
- C El Salvador
- D Senegal

08

Who was the teddy bear named after?

- A Teddy Edwards
- B Teddy Roosevelt
- C Ted Heath
- D Ted Rogers

answers turn to **w** page 116

take two

turn to page 116

09

Which county contains most of the Cotswolds?

- A Devon
- B Gloucestershire
- C Worcestershire
- D Oxfordshire

10

What does the C in CPS mean?

- A Corporation
- B Crown
- C Care
- D Clown

11

How long does pregnancy last for elephants?

- A 9 months
- B 15 months
- C 21 months
- D 28 months

12

On what charge was Joan of Arc burnt at the stake?

- A Treason
- B Murder
- C Witchcraft
- D Heresy

13

Which is the largest freshwater lake in the world?

- A Windemere
- B Superior
- C Victoria
- D Tanganyika

14

Which is Europe's highest mountain?

- A Mont Blanc
- B Matterhorn
- C Elbrus
- D Monte Cassino

15

What is the majority religion of Japan?

- A Buddhism
- B Christianity
- C Shintoism
- D Confucianism

16

Which natural landmark has had its name changed to Uluru?

- A Mount Fuji
- B Ayers Rock
- C Niagara Falls
- D The Grand Canyon

answers

turn to page 116

17
What is the term for applying medical knowledge to the law?

- A Pathology
- B Criminology
- C Forensics
- D Physiology

18
Kiev is the capital of which Eastern European country?

- A Bosnia
- B Georgia
- C Ukraine
- D Poland

19
The Watergate scandal involved which US president?

- A Richard Nixon
- B Jimmy Carter
- C Ronald Reagan
- D George Bush

20
Where did Fidel Castro become ruler in 1959?

- A Colombia
- B Cuba
- C Chile
- D Cyprus

21
How many dominoes are there in a set?

- A 68
- B 42
- C 36
- D 28

22
Whose murder led to the outbreak of World War I?

- A Kaiser Wilhelm II
- B Archduke Ferdinand
- C King George V
- D Tsar Nicholas II

23
Which film character stalked the resort of Amity Island?

- A Freddy Krueger
- B Godzilla
- C Jaws
- D King Kong

24
Where are the headquarters of the United Nations?

- A Brussels
- B Tokyo
- C New York
- D Rome

answers turn to **page 116**

turn to page 116

25

What is the British equivalent of an American zip code?

- ◆ A Pin number
- ◆ B Area code
- ◆ C Post code
- ◆ D National insurance number

26

Which is the most northern capital city in the world?

- ◆ A Reykjavik, Iceland
- ◆ B Moscow, Russia
- ◆ C Ottawa, Canada
- ◆ D Oslo, Norway

27

The Statue of Liberty was a gift to America from which country?

- ◆ A Britain
- ◆ B France
- ◆ C Germany
- ◆ D Russia

28

What is the longest side of a triangle always called?

- ◆ A Hypotenuse
- ◆ B Pythagoras
- ◆ C Isosceles
- ◆ D Appendices

29

In which month does the Chinese New Year begin?

- ◆ A January
- ◆ B February
- ◆ C March
- ◆ D April

30

What is the main ingredient of hummous?

- ◆ A Lentils
- ◆ B Chickpeas
- ◆ C Cumin
- ◆ D Cornflour

31

Who was Prime Minister at the start of World War II?

- ◆ A Neville Chamberlain
- ◆ B Winston Churchill
- ◆ C Harold Macmillan
- ◆ D David Lloyd George

32

In archery, what colour is the bullseye?

- ◆ A Red
- ◆ B Black
- ◆ C Gold
- ◆ D Blue

turn to page 116

turn to page 116

33
What does a lexicographer do?

- A Draw maps
- B Compile dictionaries
- C Analyse artwork
- D Plot graphs

34
Which chemical compound has the symbol O_3?

- A Ozone
- B Oxide
- C Osmium
- D Xenon

35
What was Mahatma Gandhi's profession?

- A Doctor
- B Lawyer
- C Politician
- D Journalist

36
In which continent are the countries Surinam and Guyana?

- A Asia
- B Africa
- C South America
- D Australasia

37
Of which country is Islamabad the capital city?

- A Pakistan
- B Iran
- C Sri Lanka
- D Turkey

38
How many sides does a dodecagon have?

- A 10
- B 12
- C 20
- D 24

39
What does a farrier do for a living?

- A Shoe horses
- B Make fences
- C Mend roofs
- D Carve wood

40
Where is the Napa Valley?

- A Morocco
- B Mexico
- C USA
- D Australia

turn to page 116

41

What does an alchemist try to do?

- A Turn metal into gold
- B Influence weather patterns
- C Find a cure for cancer
- D Conjure up the devil

42

Which part of the human body is affected by encephalitis?

- A The bladder
- B The large intestine
- C The brain
- D The lung

43

What is the term for a young female racehorse?

- A A gelding
- B A colt
- C A filly
- D A mare

44

Who has had UK No. 1 singles in each of the past five decades?

- A Elvis Presley
- B Cliff Richard
- C The Beatles
- D Frank Sinatra

45

What was the lunar module that first landed on the moon called?

- A Apollo
- B Eagle
- C Sputnik
- D Probe

46

Where do Walloons come from?

- A Luxembourg
- B Holland
- C Belgium
- D Switzerland

47

What, in 1981, had the largest TV audience in British history?

- A Falklands War broadcast
- B Star Wars TV premiere
- C Royal wedding
- D FA Cup Final

48

What is the study of codes called?

- A Enigmology
- B Cryptology
- C Numerology
- D Egyptology

49
Which African country's civil war involved the Hutus and theTutsis?

- A Nigeria
- B Senegal
- C Rwanda
- D Ethiopia

50
A langoustine can be a large example of which sea creature?

- A Oyster
- B Lobster
- C Prawn
- D Seahorse

51
What was the capital of England before London?

- A York
- B Winchester
- C Oxford
- D Worksop

52
Which minority religion is still practised in Haiti?

- A Druidism
- B Mormonism
- C Voodoo
- D Aesthism

53
Which is the largest of the Channel Islands?

- A Jersey
- B Guernsey
- C Alderney
- D Sark

54
What nationality was William Tell?

- A German
- B British
- C Austrian
- D Swiss

55
Whose ship was named 'Endeavour'?

- A Columbus
- B Raleigh
- C Cook
- D Maxwell

56
What do we call the vessels that carry blood to the heart?

- A Arteries
- B Capillaries
- C Veins
- D Alveoli

turn to page 116

57
What kind of transport is a funicular?

- A A cable car
- B A train
- C A hovercraft
- D A hot-air balloon

58
What does a philatelist collect?

- A Football programmes
- B Art
- C Stamps
- D Records

59
What did the Lumière brothers invent?

- A Phonograph
- B Cinematograph
- C Pictograph
- D Telegraph

60
What is the lightest weight division in professional boxing?

- A Welterweight
- B Strawweight
- C Bantamweight
- D Featherweight

61
Which river runs through the Grand Canyon?

- A Mississippi
- B Colorado
- C Columbia
- D Missouri

62
Which Hollywood actress became a Monaco princess?

- A Eva Marie Saint
- B Grace Kelly
- C Marilyn Monroe
- D Ingrid Bergman

63
What name was given to Hitler's planned invasion of Britain?

- A Seawolf
- B Sealion
- C Seahorse
- D Seashark

64
Which region of North-east Spain has Barcelona as its capital?

- A Grenada
- B Catalonia
- C Valencia
- D Basque

turn to page 116

turn to page 116

65
In which continent
is the Gobi desert?

- A Australasia
- B Asia
- C South America
- D Africa

66
What does a
lepidopterist collect?

- A Butterflies
- B Film posters
- C Money
- D Magazines

67
What colour
is vermillion?

- A Greenish-blue
- B Reddish-orange
- C Pinkish-white
- D Yellowish-green

68
In which decade was
the book '1984' written?

- A 1920s
- B 1940s
- C 1960s
- D 1980s

69
Which dog breed shares the
name of Charles Darwin's ship?

- A Dalmatian
- B Spaniel
- C Beagle
- D Terrier

70
On which continent are
the Atlas mountains?

- A Asia
- B Africa
- C North America
- D South America

71
Which salad contains walnuts
apples, celery and mayonnaise?

- A Nicoise
- B Waldorf
- C Greek
- D Farmhouse

72
Super G is an event
in which sport?

- A Rallying
- B Skiing
- C Cycling
- D Motorcycling

73
What does the Latin phrase 'carpe diem' mean?

- ◆ A Never look back
- ◆ B Sieze the day
- ◆ C Follow your heart
- ◆ D Drive carefully

74
Cagliari is the capital city of which Mediterranean island?

- ◆ A Majorca
- ◆ B Sardinia
- ◆ C Corsica
- ◆ D Crete

75
Which Italian city has a football club called Juventus?

- ◆ A Rome
- ◆ B Milan
- ◆ C Turin
- ◆ D Naples

76
In 1853, what was George Crum the first chef to serve?

- ◆ A Chips
- ◆ B Crisps
- ◆ C Biscuits
- ◆ D Toast

77
How old was Boris Becker when he first won Wimbledon?

- ◆ A 16
- ◆ B 17
- ◆ C 18
- ◆ D 19

78
What is the Dutch national airline called?

- ◆ A Go
- ◆ B KLM
- ◆ C Lufthansa
- ◆ D QANTAS

79
What does 'cosa nostra' literally mean?

- ◆ A In the family
- ◆ B Our affair
- ◆ C Organized crime
- ◆ D Open house

80
What is an archipelago?

- ◆ A A group of houses
- ◆ B A group of islands
- ◆ C A group of lakes
- ◆ D A group of shops

answers

turn to   page 116

take two

Check your options to the questions below

page 106	page 107	page 108	page 109	page 110
◆ 01 AC	◆ 09 BD	◆ 17 BC	◆ 25 AC	◆ 33 AB
◆ 02 BC	◆ 10 AB	◆ 18 CD	◆ 26 AC	◆ 34 AC
◆ 03 AB	◆ 11 BC	◆ 19 AB	◆ 27 BD	◆ 35 AB
◆ 04 BD	◆ 12 BD	◆ 20 AB	◆ 28 AC	◆ 36 BC
◆ 05 AD	◆ 13 BC	◆ 21 BD	◆ 29 BC	◆ 37 AB
◆ 06 BD	◆ 14 AC	◆ 22 AB	◆ 30 AB	◆ 38 BC
◆ 07 AC	◆ 15 AC	◆ 23 BC	◆ 31 AB	◆ 39 AC
◆ 08 AB	◆ 16 AB	◆ 24 AC	◆ 32 BC	◆ 40 AC

page 111	page 112	page 113	page 114	page 115
◆ 41 AB	◆ 49 BC	◆ 57 BD	◆ 65 BC	◆ 73 BC
◆ 42 CD	◆ 50 BC	◆ 58 BC	◆ 66 AB	◆ 74 BC
◆ 43 AC	◆ 51 AB	◆ 59 AB	◆ 67 AB	◆ 75 AC
◆ 44 AB	◆ 52 AC	◆ 60 BD	◆ 68 BC	◆ 76 AB
◆ 45 BC	◆ 53 AB	◆ 61 BD	◆ 69 AC	◆ 77 BC
◆ 46 AC	◆ 54 CD	◆ 62 AB	◆ 70 AB	◆ 78 AB
◆ 47 BC	◆ 55 AC	◆ 63 AB	◆ 71 AB	◆ 79 BD
◆ 48 BC	◆ 56 AC	◆ 64 AB	◆ 72 BD	◆ 80 BD

answers

page 106	page 107	page 108	page 109	page 110
◆ 01 C	◆ 09 B	◆ 17 C	◆ 25 C	◆ 33 B
◆ 02 C	◆ 10 B	◆ 18 C	◆ 26 A	◆ 34 A
◆ 03 A	◆ 11 B	◆ 19 A	◆ 27 B	◆ 35 B
◆ 04 B	◆ 12 D	◆ 20 B	◆ 28 A	◆ 36 C
◆ 05 D	◆ 13 C	◆ 21 D	◆ 29 B	◆ 37 A
◆ 06 D	◆ 14 C	◆ 22 B	◆ 30 B	◆ 38 B
◆ 07 C	◆ 15 C	◆ 23 C	◆ 31 A	◆ 39 A
◆ 08 B	◆ 16 B	◆ 24 C	◆ 32 C	◆ 40 C

page 111	page 112	page 113	page 114	page 115
◆ 41 A	◆ 49 C	◆ 57 B	◆ 65 B	◆ 73 B
◆ 42 C	◆ 50 C	◆ 58 C	◆ 66 A	◆ 74 B
◆ 43 C	◆ 51 B	◆ 59 B	◆ 67 B	◆ 75 C
◆ 44 B	◆ 52 C	◆ 60 B	◆ 68 B	◆ 76 B
◆ 45 B	◆ 53 A	◆ 61 B	◆ 69 C	◆ 77 B
◆ 46 C	◆ 54 D	◆ 62 B	◆ 70 B	◆ 78 B
◆ 47 C	◆ 55 C	◆ 63 B	◆ 71 B	◆ 79 B
◆ 48 B	◆ 56 C	◆ 64 B	◆ 72 B	◆ 80 B

level
ten

taketwo

turn to page 128

01

In which country is the city of Mecca?

- A Jordan
- B Israel
- C Saudi Arabia
- D Oman

02

In which country is the River Ganges?

- A China
- B India
- C The Philippines
- D Kenya

03

If it's midday in Britain in May, what is the time in New York?

- A 1am
- B 7am
- C 5pm
- D 9pm

04

During whose reign was the phrase 'your majesty' first used?

- A Henry VIII
- B Charles I
- C George II
- D Victoria I

05

What's the capital city of Bavaria?

- A Munich
- B Hamburg
- C Frankfurt
- D Dresden

06

What country is called Suomi by its people?

- A Iceland
- B Greenland
- C Finland
- D Sweden

07

Which bird supplies the feathers for a traditional shuttlecock?

- A A signet
- B A gannet
- C A goose
- D An ostrich

08

How long ago did dinosaurs become extinct?

- A 10 million years
- B 30 million years
- C 65 million years
- D 90 million years

answers

turn to page 128

09

What was the name of 1998's sound-barrier-breaking car?

- A Force
- B Probe
- C Thrust
- D Impetus

10

What was originally thought to be the cause of malaria?

- A Rats
- B Mouldy bread
- C Bad smells
- D A voodoo curse

11

What is thought to have been the loudest noise known to man?

- A Hiroshima bombing
- B Gansu earthquake, China
- C Krakatoa eruption
- D The Big Bang

12

Which cartoon character made his debut in 'Steamboat Willie'?

- A Donald Duck
- B Mickey Mouse
- C Bugs Bunny
- D Popeye

13

How long ago did humans begin to hunt, fish, and develop tools?

- A 5 million years
- B 2.7 million years
- C 500,000 years
- D 40,000 years

14

An auction where the bidding starts high is called what?

- A A Spanish auction
- B A French auction
- C A Dutch auction
- D A Russian auction

15

What is the layer that lies under the earth's crust called?

- A The silicate
- B The mantle
- C The inner crust
- D The lithosphere

16

Who killed Billy the Kid?

- A Pat Garret
- B Wyatt Earp
- C Butch Cassidy
- D The Lone Ranger

answers

turn to   page 128

119

take two

turn to page 128

17
Which city has the world's longest underground network?

- A Paris
- B New York
- C London
- D Tokyo

18
Which country owned Florida before the USA?

- A Britain
- B Spain
- C Russia
- D Cuba

19
How many people attended the 1950 World Cup Final?

- A 144,000
- B 176,000
- C 199,000
- D 220,000

20
Who won the Battle of Little Bighorn?

- A Sioux Indians
- B Unionists
- C Independents
- D Apache Indians

21
Which creature uses a 'Jacobson's organ' to smell?

- A An aardvark
- B A snake
- C A dog
- D A fly

22
Which English town was most severely damaged in the Blitz?

- A Ipswich
- B Sunderland
- C Coventry
- D London

23
The Suez canal connects which two seas?

- A Caspian and Arabian
- B Black and South China
- C Irish and North
- D Mediterranean and Red

24
Which of the body's senses involves the olfactory nerves?

- A Touch
- B Taste
- C Hearing
- D Smell

answers

turn to page 128

turn to page 128

25
Which is the biggest city in China?

- A Beijing
- B Hong Kong
- C Macao
- D Shanghai

26
What kind of architecture is Notre Dame an example of?

- A Classical
- B Renaissance
- C Gothic
- D Art Deco

27
What does Thailand literally mean?

- A Land of the Sun
- B Land of the Chosen
- C Land of the Free
- D Land of the Tourist

28
Which landmark has a 365-foot dome?

- A St. Paul's Cathedral
- B The Millennium Dome
- C The Sistine Chapel
- D The Epcot Centre

29
How deep is the ocean at its deepest trench?

- A Ten miles
- B Seven miles
- C Two miles
- D Five miles

30
Which 17th century king built the Palace of Versailles?

- A Louis XIII
- B Louis XIV
- C Louis XV
- D Louis XVI

31
What was the world population in 2000?

- A 4.4 billion
- B 6.2 billion
- C 9.5 billion
- D 14.3 billion

32
Roughly how far is the Earth from the Sun?

- A 900,000 miles
- B 9 million miles
- C 90 million miles
- D 900 million miles

turn to page 128

turn to page 128

33
What was the 1927 film 'The Jazz Singer' the first to use?

- A Music
- B Swearing
- C Sound
- D Women

34
When Columbus landed in Cuba, where did he think he was?

- A America
- B Japan
- C China
- D India

35
In which two South American countries is Patagonia?

- A Brazil and Peru
- B Argentina and Chile
- C Venezuela and Uruguay
- D Paraguay and Colombia

36
US state names most commonly end in which letter?

- A N
- B Y
- C A
- D R

37
What is the lowest ranking suit in the card game bridge?

- A Hearts
- B Diamonds
- C Clubs
- D Spades

38
What is Aurora Borealis better known as?

- A Halley's Comet
- B A shooting star
- C The Northern Lights
- D A black hole

39
Whose brain was sliced into 34,000 segments for analysis?

- A Lenin's
- B Albert Einstein's
- C Emperor Hirohito's
- D Adolf Hitler's

40
Which sea is the biggest?

- A Caribbean
- B Mediterranean
- C South China
- D Bering

turn to page 128

take two

turn to page 128

41
Which is the world's widest river?

- A Nile
- B Rhine
- C Amazon
- D Mississippi

42
New York stands on the banks of which river?

- A Lawrence
- B Delaware
- C Hudson
- D Newark

43
Which British islands are the most northerly?

- A The Shetlands Islands
- B Orkneys
- C Outer Hebrides
- D Scilly Isles

44
Which sea lies between Italy and Croatia?

- A Mediterranean
- B Tyrrhenian
- C Adriatic
- D Ionian

45
Who is the Aga Khan?

- A A political leader
- B A religious leader
- C A military leader
- D A community leader

46
In which decade was the film '2001: A Space Odyssey' made?

- A 1950s
- B 1960s
- C 1970s
- D 1980s

47
Which island republic lies off the east coast of Africa?

- A Sri Lanka
- B Madagascar
- C Borneo
- D New Guinea

48
What do the thirteen stripes on the US flag represent?

- A The first thirteen presidents
- B The thirteen amendments
- C The thirteen original states
- D The thirteen Pilgrim Fathers

answers turn to page 128

49
What is the capital city of Venezuela?

- A La Paz
- B Lima
- C Santiago
- D Caracas

50
Which writer's name now implies cunning and opportunism?

- A Swift
- B Bufalino
- C Machiavelli
- D Vidal

51
Which crop does the boll weevil infest?

- A Cotton
- B Wheat
- C Corn
- D Maize

52
Who was the first king of England?

- A Ethelred
- B Athelstan
- C Alfred
- D Egbert

53
Which artist's surname was Buonarotti?

- A Canaletto
- B Donatello
- C Michelangelo
- D Caravaggio

54
Which is Europe's longest river?

- A Danube
- B Volga
- C Dnieper
- D Rhine

55
How long did the Hundred Years War last?

- A 96 years
- B 101 years
- C 108 years
- D 116 years

56
Where was Wenceslas the king of?

- A Mesopotamia
- B Israel
- C Bohemia
- D Norway

57

How many hills is Rome built upon?

- ◆A Two
- ◆B Four
- ◆C Seven
- ◆D Ten

58

Manila is the capital city of which country?

- ◆A Thailand
- ◆B Vietnam
- ◆C The Philippines
- ◆D Malaysia

59

A prototype of which sea vessel was invented in 1620?

- ◆A The hovercraft
- ◆B The submarine
- ◆C The passenger liner
- ◆D The speed boat

60

What did Alfred Nobel invent in 1867?

- ◆A The motor boat
- ◆B Fingerprinting
- ◆C Dynamite
- ◆D The water pistol

61

How long is the Great Wall of China?

- ◆A 80 miles
- ◆B 560 miles
- ◆C 1,500 miles
- ◆D 4,700 miles

62

Which country was called Helvetia in Latin?

- ◆A Switzerland
- ◆B Spain
- ◆C France
- ◆D Germany

63

Who must take the Hippocratic Oath?

- ◆A Doctors
- ◆B Soldiers
- ◆C Politicians
- ◆D Policemen

64

What is a smorgasbord?

- ◆A A buffet meal
- ◆B A gangplank
- ◆C A steam bath
- ◆D A Nordic chalet

answers
turn to page 128

65
Who became the first leader of the Scottish Assembly in 1999?

- A John Menzies-Campbell
- B Donald Dewar
- C Alex Salmond
- D Gordon Brown

66
Who wrote the book 'Chitty, Chitty, Bang, Bang'?

- A Roald Dahl
- B Ian Fleming
- C Walt Disney
- D Dick Van Dyke

67
What is the average human said to do 2.5 million times a year?

- A Breathe
- B Take a step
- C Swallow
- D Think

68
Which country is the world's biggest exporter of gold?

- A South Africa
- B Argentina
- C Russia
- D China

69
How many miles long is the equator?

- A 11,587 miles
- B 18,246 miles
- C 24,902 miles
- D 29,391 miles

70
When did London become the capital of England?

- A 178
- B 745
- C 1066
- D 1357

71
Where did King George II die?

- A On a battlefield
- B In a duel
- C In prison
- D On a toilet

72
What is the world's third largest country?

- A Russia
- B China
- C Greenland
- D Australia

73
The Brenner pass goes through which mountain range?

- A The Himalayas
- B The Andes
- C The Alps
- D The Pyrenees

74
What was the minimum age for working children in 1833?

- A Six
- B Nine
- C Twelve
- D Fifteen

75
What killed 20 million people in 1918?

- A World War One
- B Famine
- C Influenza
- D Heart disease

76
How many earths would fit into Jupiter?

- A 4
- B 77
- C 376
- D 1300

77
What does the R in RPI stand for?

- A Revenue
- B Retail
- C Register
- D Resources

78
In which year was the internet originated?

- A 1945
- B 1969
- C 1978
- D 1991

79
What was Bangladesh formerly called?

- A Kashmir
- B East Pakistan
- C Bengal
- D East India

80
What are the twenty regions of Paris called?

- A Départements
- B Arrondissements
- C Séctions
- D Localités

 answers
turn to   page 128

127

take two

Check your options to the questions below

answers